SEVEN BOOKS OF WISDOM

Seven Books of Wisdom is one of the volumes in a new series, IMPACT BOOKS, designed to bring to the modern reader the significant achievements of scholars, both Catholic and non-Catholic, in the fields of Scripture, Theology, Philosophy, Mathematics, History, and the Physical and Social Sciences. IMPACT BOOKS will explore these realms of human knowledge in order to give the average man some idea of the work being carried on today within them and in order to lay a basis for fruitful dialogue between men of different interests and persuasions on questions vital to all mankind.

SEVEN BOOKS
OF
WISDOM

✝

Roland E. Murphy, O.Carm.

PROFESSOR OF OLD TESTAMENT
THE CATHOLIC UNIVERSITY OF AMERICA

THE BRUCE PUBLISHING COMPANY
MILWAUKEE

223.07

MuS

IMPRIMI POTEST:

> RAPHAEL P. KIEFFER, O.CARM.
> *Prior Provincialis*

NIHIL OBSTAT:

> WILLIAM N. SCHUIT
> *Censor deputatus*

IMPRIMATUR:

> ✠ WILLIAM E. COUSINS
> *Archbishop of Milwaukee*
> July 13, 1960

Library of Congress Catalog Card Number: 60–14446

To My Mother

PREFACE

The author of Proverbs tells his readers:

> Say to Wisdom, "You are my sister!"
> Call Understanding, "Friend!" (Prv 7:4.)

The present volume is designed to echo this invitation by presenting an introduction to the Sapiential Books of the Old Testament. The appearance of the splendid modern translation of these books in the CCD (Confraternity of Christian Doctrine) version of 1955 prompts this companion volume which aims to provide the background and explanation of a literature so remote from our own times and mentality. Without such guidance one may fear that the average reader will neglect the priceless heritage of Hebrew wisdom literature.

We use the phrase "Sapiential Books" in the sense in which it was applied in early Christianity, when it was used to embrace more than the accepted and narrower list of Proverbs, Job, Ecclesiastes, Sirach, and Wisdom. Hence we include the Psalms and the Canticle of Canticles. Moreover, we call attention to the inclusion of Sirach and Wisdom, which are classed among the Apocrypha by our non-Catholic brethren. Our list could have been expanded to Baruch and other small pieces of wisdom literature, but the line had to be drawn somewhere, and the traditional seven "Sapiential Books" seem a satisfactory number.

It is worth stating the conviction that this is not a "terminal" book. The reader may not close this book with any degree of success or satisfaction, unless he has already opened his Old Testament as an accompaniment. Ideally, this is a *companion* volume for one who wants to read these seven Old Testament compositions. It gives the necessary introduction to the historical background and type of literature exemplified by these works, along with an interpretation of their message. There are many complex problems associated with the wisdom literature which are not treated; but in a work of this sort they are best left unexplored, even if indicated.

This popular presentation of the wisdom literature has grown out of the survey courses which the author has conducted at the Carmelite theological seminary, Whitefriars Hall, at the school of theology of the Catholic University of America, and at the University of Notre Dame. While he alone bears the responsibility for what is written here, he wishes to acknowledge a great debt to the labors of many who have wrestled with these books, and the expert in the field will recognize this indebtedness readily enough. But most of all he is indebted to the Confraternity of Christian Doctrine translation — for a good translation is already a quasi-commentary. He was privileged to have worked on the editorial board of this translation and, in particular, to have benefited from the insights of his colleague and former teacher, Rt. Rev. Monsignor Patrick W. Skehan, vice-chairman of the board. Without the new CCD translation this book would not have been written; with it, this book will serve, it is hoped, as a not unworthy introduction to the wisdom of Israel.

ROLAND E. MURPHY, O.CARM.

CONTENTS

The Books of the Old Testament
And Their Abbreviations

Genesis	Gn	Ecclesiastes	Eccl
Exodus	Ex	Canticle of Canticles	Ct
Leviticus	Lv	Wisdom	Wis
Numbers	Nm	Sirach (Ecclesiasticus)	Sir
Deuteronomy	Dt	Isaias	Is
Josue	Jos	Jeremias	Jer
Judges	Jgs	Lamentations	Lam
Ruth	Ru	Baruch	Bar
1 Samuel (Kings)	1 Sm	Ezechiel	Ez
2 Samuel (Kings)	2 Sm	Daniel	Dn
3 Kings	3 Kgs	Osee	Os
4 Kings	4 Kgs	Joel	Jl
1 Paralipomenon (Chronicles)	1 Par	Amos	Am
		Abdias	Abd
2 Paralipomenon (Chronicles)	2 Par	Jonas	Jon
Esdras	Esd	Micheas	Mi
Nehemias (2 Esdras)	Neh	Nahum	Na
Tobias	Tb	Habacuc	Hb
Judith	Jdt	Sophonias	So
Esther	Est	Aggeus	Ag
Job	Jb	Zacharias	Za
Psalms	Ps(s)	Malachias	Mal
Proverbs	Prv	1 Machabees	1 Mc
		2 Machabees	2 Mc

SEVEN BOOKS OF WISDOM

1. HEBREW POETRY

When the reader takes up the so-called Sapiential Books of the Old Testament, a certain orientation is helpful. All of these books, with the exception of portions of Proverbs and many of the Psalms, were written after the Babylonian exile (587–539 B.C.). Although the classical era of Hebrew literature was at an end, the dialogue in Job is equal to the high level of the best Hebrew poetry. For want of a better word, we might classify the general content of these books as a practical philosophy, an expression of the ideals and aspirations that motivated the Jews in their daily living. The Hebrew was not philosophical in the sense that he reasoned speculatively about things, but he had certain definite ideas about God and man and life and these ideas will not escape the careful reader.

Very often it will be necessary to shed preconceived ideas. This is particularly true for the Christian, who is tempted to read the Old Testament on a level with the New, and to discover the ideas of the New in the Old. To do this is to forget the proper relationship between the Old and the New, to forget that divine revelation was gradual. There is a remarkable divine "condescension" in revelation, as the Fathers of the Church noted in their commentaries and homilies on Scripture. This means that God took his Chosen People *as they were*. There was no revolutionary change in them. Polygamy, for example, was practiced, and there is no divine legislation against it. Abraham, Moses, and the prophets did not become Christian saints by virtue of their experience with God. This does not mean that there was no change wrought in them or that their experience of God was negligible. Rather, the simple fact is that we must evaluate them honestly against their own background and

1

resources; we cannot transfer them into the framework of our times and views.

Parallelism

An appreciation of the characteristics of Hebrew poetry is essential for an intelligent reading of the wisdom literature of the Old Testament. We might begin by observing that Hebrew poetry lacks rhymed verse, or the alternation of long and short vowels; in this respect it resembles somewhat our blank verse. The essential note of Hebrew poetry (in prophetical as well as sapiential literature) is parallelism, a thought rhythm and not a vowel rhythm.

The classical study on Hebrew parallelism was done by an eighteenth-century Anglican bishop, Robert Lowth. He defined parallelism as a certain equality or similarity between the two parts or members of a sentence; the words in these parts correspond to each other. The first member raises a certain expectation, and the second satisfies or completes it:

> Have mercy on me, O God, in your goodness;
>   in the greatness of your compassion wipe out my offense
>
> (Ps 51:3).

One looks, therefore, to a group of lines, not single lines, as the key to poetic expression. Unfortunately, not enough editors and publishers of Bibles pay attention to this elementary fact. Their tendency is to block the verses together according to their numerical sequence, with no regard for the balance of ideas expressed within a verse. Prose and poetry are treated as if there were no difference between them. The result makes for an unpleasant format as well as an obscuring of the author's ideas. The reader can test this for himself by comparing the versification of the CCD translation (at least, as originally published by the St. Anthony Guild Press) with the traditional Douay-Rheims versification in the poetical books; or one can compare the new Revised Standard Version (of the National Council of the Churches of Christ) with the traditional format of the King James version.

Although there are many forms of parallelism, three types are most frequent: synonymous, antithetic, and synthetic. *Synonymous* parallelism means that the second member or line repeats the idea of the first with some slight variation. Thus, Psalm 38 begins:

> O Lord, in your anger punish me not,
> in your wrath chastise me not. . . .

The second line repeats the idea of the first with different words.

Antithetic parallelism presents a contrast between two members; ultimately they say the same thing, but by way of negation or contrast. An example is Proverbs:

> A wise son makes his father glad,
> but a foolish son is grief to his mother (10:1).

Synthetic parallelism is really a broad category which includes those types of parallelism which cannot be classified as synonymous or antithetic. A parallelism in the sense of the expectation mentioned above is to be found here, although it is not as tractable as the first two types. Thus, Job says of God:

> Yet he knows my way;
> if he proved me, I should come forth as gold (23:10).

The first line raises a certain expectation: Is Job's way good or bad? The second line answers, but not by any real parallelism of thought; it goes beyond the first line. Another example of synthetic parallelism has been given its own picturesque name, "staircase" parallelism; each of the first two lines builds up to the third, as in Psalm 92:10,

> For behold, your enemies, O Lord,
> for behold, your enemies shall perish;
> all evildoers shall be scattered.

This verse is of particular interest because it has been certainly influenced by, if not borrowed from, the literature of ancient Ugarit (modern Ras Shamra in Syria). In the cycle of the famous Ugaritic epic, Baal and Anat, a messenger addresses Baal:

> Behold, your enemies, O Baal,
>   Behold, your enemies you will smite;
>   Behold, you will vanquish your foes (Gordon 68:8).

The same "staircase" parallelism and the same ideas are found in this Ugaritic verse. Many more examples of the influence of Ugaritic literature on Old Testament poetry could be adduced, but here we wish merely to call attention to parallelism as the striking characteristic of Hebrew and all ancient Semitic verse.

Parallelism can be further analyzed in view of the variations of rhythm within a verse, but the three essential types listed above are sufficient for one who wants to read Old Testament poetry with some artistic appreciation. Moreover, the phenomenon of parallelism is important for understanding the meaning of the verse. Sometimes the meaning of either member is somewhat vague, but the key to the understanding can be supplied by the other member, as in Wisdom 4:9,

> Rather, understanding is the hoary crown for men,
>   and an unsullied life, the attainment of old age.

The "hoary crown" is made clear by its counterpart, "the attainment of old age."

The Gnomic Saying, or Proverb

Within our own English literature we are aware of various types of poetry, such as lyric, epic, didactic, etc., which are classified by content, mood, style, and pattern of versification. Hebrew literature is likewise varied; we have several clearly recognizable types scattered throughout the Bible. The forty-seventh chapter of Isaias contains a mocking song in which the prophet jeers at Babylon. He ridicules her divinities, Bel and Nebo, who are carried into exile. A touching example of a funeral song or elegy is David's lament over the dead Saul and Jonathan (2 Sm 1:19–27), and the Book of Lamentations is an excellent imitation of the funeral song. It is generally recognized that Numbers 21:17 ff., "the song of the well," is a working song, or at least modeled on that pattern. The "eat and drink, for tomorrow we die" in Isaias 22:13 seems to be a snatch of a drinking song which the prophet is quoting. As we shall see in detail, the Canticle of Canticles contains wedding songs, and the Psalter is made up of several definite types of songs, such as hymns of praise, laments, royal songs, etc.

Against this rich literary background the proverbial or gnomic saying stands out as being the primary characteristic, the vehicle in fact, of a large portion of the wisdom literature (Prv, Eccl, Sir, Wis). The Hebrew term is *mashal*, traditionally translated as "proverb," but this is much more inclusive than our "proverb." It is used to designate jibes and derisory statements, such as "where is now your God?" (Ps 42:4, 11) or the magnificent satire on the king of Babylon in Isaias 14. Perhaps the most satisfactory explanation that has been offered for *mashal* is that it means "comparison." At least this accounts for the frequent comparisons that are found:

> It is better to dwell in a corner of a housetop
> than in a roomy house with a quarrelsome woman
>
> (Prv 25:24).

In any case, the typical *mashal*, such as is found in the *Mishle Shelomoh* (Proverbs of Solomon), reflects ideas on various aspects of human affairs. These are attained by observing a succession of events and experiences. Hence they will formulate a sort of "law" which introduces order into the welter of human activities. After a number of occurrences one can formulate the conclusion:

> Pride goes before disaster
> and a haughty spirit before a fall (Prv 16:18; cf. 18:12).

This observation is not dictated primarily by religious considerations; it is a fact which the wise man can verify by citing instances.

However, many features of human life will not submit to easy conclusions; among them are paradoxes:

> One man is lavish yet grows still richer;
> another is too sparing, yet is the poorer (Prv 11:24).

This is simply an observation and it records the fact without any attempt at explanation. The Sages recognized many such paradoxes: love of a child means chastising him (Prv 13:24); bitter is sweet to the hungry man (Prv 27:7). Riddles, too, figure in these observations, as in the comparison between a man who boastfully promises something, and clouds which give no rain (Prv 25:14). These comparisons between events of nature and human activity are frequent; they represent the two worlds man is trying to cope with:

> As iron sharpens iron,
>   so man sharpens his fellow man (Prv 27:17).

Besides the proverb, whether a single unit as in Proverbs or developed into a series of observations as in Sirach, an admonishing tone is characteristic of this literature. The wisdom teacher addresses his pupil as "my son," and bids him "listen," "beware," etc. The admonition is another indication that Old Testament wisdom literature is essentially didactic in character. The object is not a speculative, scientific, or psychological insight into human affairs; the aim is much more practical: to indoctrinate young men with the body of wisdom that has accumulated over the years. That is why table etiquette as well as religious insights are included in the program of the wise man. Really, nothing in human life would be without relevance to this program: women, money, speech, dealings with one's neighbor. It is remarkable that this complete body of teaching has been composed almost without any reference to specific items of Israel's cult or history. From this point of view, the wisdom teaching manifests the most universal aspect of the Old Testament. It is not consciously nationalistic as the Law and the Prophets clearly are. A fatherly attitude has replaced the "Thus says the Lord" of the prophetical period.

As one might expect, the vocabulary of the wisdom literature is somewhat specialized. The synonyms of wisdom (ḥokmah) may be instanced: understanding (binah); prudence (sekel); cunning ('ormah), etc. It is often difficult to distinguish between them, but the context will help. These terms indicate what has to be learned by the "simple" (*peti*) who is easily deceived, by the fool (*'ewil*) who is given over to folly, by the stupid (*kesil*) who lacks sense, by the malicious fool (*nabal*), by the mocker (*leṣ*), etc. Modern readers must realize that these terms do not have the intellectual connotation which we generally ascribe to them. Wisdom and folly are essentially directed toward one's relationship to God, toward moral conduct. In the Old Testament the wise man is not an intellectual; he is a religious man who lives up to his obligations to God and man; the fool is not necessarily mentally stupid; he refuses to serve God, and such a course is folly by Old Testament standards.

2. PROVERBS:
THE SAYINGS OF THE SCRIBES

THE book of Proverbs is one of the most deceptive of the Old Testament because it seems to be understood so easily. Aside from a few obscure sayings, everything is rather cut and dried. What more obvious than

> A wise son makes his father glad,
> but a foolish son is a grief to his mother (10:1)?

Even if there are some deep and weighty observations, the stated purpose of the book is almost disarming:

> That men may appreciate wisdom and discipline,
> may understand words of intelligence;
> May receive training in wise conduct,
> in what is right, just and honest;
> That resourcefulness may be imparted to the simple,
> to the young man knowledge and discretion (1:2–4).

One might gather from these words that Proverbs is just another "good book." But that would be to miss the dramatic and dynamic purpose of the architect of this book, which is revealed in the first nine chapters that he composed as an introduction. It would also be to miss the true import of the various collections of proverbs which he assembled and edited.

The divisions of the book of Proverbs are more important than is the case with most other biblical works. The dividing lines have been deliberately inserted, and they serve to warn us that the book is essentially a *collection* of sayings: those of Solomon (10:1;

25:1), the Wise (or the Sages) (22:17; 24:23), Agur (30:1), and Lamuel (31:1). To this collection of primarily pre-exilic material the compiler, a postexilic sage, provides an introduction (cc. 1–9). Thus we have the following division:

    I: Introduction: The Value of Wisdom (1:1–9:18)

    II: First Collection of the Proverbs of Solomon (10:1–22:16)

    III: Sayings of the Wise (22:17–24:22)

    IV: Other Sayings of the Wise (24:23–34)

    V: Second Collection of the Proverbs of Solomon (25:1–29:27)

    VI: The Words of Agur (30:1–14)

    VII: Numerical Proverbs (30:15–33)

    VIII: The Words of Lamuel (31:1–9)

    IX: The Ideal Wife (31:10–31)

Before getting into the proverbs themselves, we must understand something of their origin and background, as well as the purpose of the compiler's introduction.

The Origin and Background of the Proverb Collection

The royal court in Jerusalem is the life-setting for the proverbs; it is here that they originated in large part, and where they were cultivated intensely by the members of the court. This association of wisdom literature with royalty is already suggested in the Bible itself, where Solomon's wisdom is described at great length (cf. 3 Kgs 4:29 ff.; 10:1 ff.). The same association is also attested in the countries surrounding Israel, with Egypt the most notable example, where we find, even in the third millennium before Christ, the Instruction of Ptah-hotep, the vizier of Pharaoh Izezi (about 2450 B.C.). The instruction follows the typical pattern of wisdom literature: a father speaking to his son, telling him what is to be looked for in an official of the court: eloquent speech, justice, etiquette while dining with the great, a sense of responsi-

bility in doing assigned work, avoiding evil women and covetous-
ness, justice to clients, a proper relationship to superiors, etc. This
type of instruction is repeated by later officials: the instruction for
King Meri-Ka-Re (by his father), the Instruction of King Amen-
em-het, the Instruction of Ani, etc. The function of this literature
is obvious: the training of youths who were to take up their re-
spective posts at court as copyists, translators, clerks, and the many
odd jobs that bureaucracy engenders. It will be recalled that the
kingdom of Israel was born of the desire to be "like all the nations"
(1 Sm 8:20). In taking over the institution of kingship, Israel
also adopted many things that went with it, particularly the court
and court life. Under Solomon a more international atmosphere
prevailed (one thinks of his marriage to Pharaoh's daughter). The
duties of courtiers multiplied: army, finance and taxes, government
executives, scribes for writing and translating. The cultivation of
"wisdom" which was found necessary for this life in Egypt was
necessary in Israel too, and the wisdom movement was on its way.
It is here that the proverb collection fits.

The titles referring to Solomon, King Lamuel and Agur reflect
this courtly background and indicate that the compiler is publishing the sayings as a collection of royal wisdom. An alert reading
will discover very many sayings which apply to the situation of
a courtier. It is according to this teaching that a young man at
court is expected to live and work out his career: discipline, correction, instruction, drinking, laziness, evil women, etc. As we have
seen, this is matched by the instructions prepared for young men
at the Egyptian court. Yet there is a profound difference, due to
the specifically Israelite stamp given to these admonitions. One
should not imagine that training for court life was exclusively
secular. In every chapter the name of Yahweh figures. Jeremias
had harsh words concerning the royal counselors of his day (Jer
8:8–9), but sages were not the only evildoers in that national
crisis. By and large, they would have been decent and loyal
Yahwists, if one judges by the sound religious advice contained in
the proverbs.

The Introduction (cc. 1–9)

The language, point of view, and dependence on earlier biblical books (especially on Dt, Jer, Is) allow us to conclude that the author of the introduction wrote after the exile (539 B.C.). He indulges in the literary process called by the late Père Robert the anthological style which consists in using the phraseology of early biblical books in order to express one's thoughts. At first sight it seems strange that a postexilic writer should perpetuate a collection of proverbs which were originally destined for royalty. The monarchy had long since disappeared; the prophetic condemnation of the people on account of national guilt had been justified by events. The fearsome exile had scattered the Jews over the world, and even in their own country they lived uneasily in the satrapy established by Persia. Was there a way, which still relied on biblical teaching and tradition, of reaching the minds and hearts of their compatriots? The wisdom movement answered this question with the distillation of the practical religious mentality of old. Despite the original purpose of these proverbs, they still had a function to perform when the monarchy was gone. Slowly the wisdom writers in the postexilic period came to identify wisdom with the Torah, or Law, as the most effective way of practical religion. The author of Proverbs 1–9 has not gone that far; instead he identifies wisdom somehow with God — it is divine. He wants to impart to his readers a very high and exalted notion of the proverbs he collected. He does this by describing the happy results of Wisdom and the disastrous consequences of Folly, and in particular by his personification and divinization of Wisdom. This treatment of Wisdom, as opposed to Dame Folly, occurs in three passages: 1:20–33; 8:1–36; 9:1–6, 13–18.

First, Wisdom assumes the role of a prophet like Jeremias, crying aloud "in the street," "at the city gates" (Jer 11:6; 17:19). But she is far more than a "wise man" or even a prophet; she is a being who has a right to speak as God and, like him, she pours forth her spirit (1:23). Isaias had described Yahweh as pouring his spirit upon the Israelites (Is 44:3). In the biblical tradition,

the pouring out of the spirit is something which belongs to God —
and here it is attributed to Wisdom. Just as Yahweh complained
that he called but Israel did not answer, that he stretched out
his hands in vain and therefore the nation is punished (Is 65:1–2;
12–13; 66:4), so Wisdom has the same experiences:

> Because I called and you refused,
>   I extended my hand and no one took notice; . . .
> I, in my turn, will laugh at your doom;
>   I will mock when terror overtakes you (1:24–26).

Wisdom speaks as one having authority, granting security to those
who obey her (1:33) and leaving fools to suffer their own fate
(1:31).

Second, Wisdom has the same effect as the "spirit of the Lord."
The spirit of the Lord that comes upon Emmanuel in Isaias 11:2
is described as a spirit of wisdom and understanding, of counsel
and strength, a spirit of knowledge. These are also the marks of
Wisdom in Proverbs:

> Mine are counsel and advice;
>   mine is strength; I am understanding (8:14).

In Job these are mentioned as attributes which are specifically
divine:

> With him [God] are wisdom and strength;
>   his are counsel and understanding (12:13).

Just as these virtues secure for Emmanuel a rule marked by justice
and right judgment (Is 11:3–5), so also they are the necessary
possession of all rulers of this world, who must cultivate wisdom:

> By me kings reign
>   and lawgivers establish justice;
> By me princes govern,
>   and nobles; all the rulers of earth (8:15 f.).

Third, like the Lord himself, Wisdom has prepared a sacrificial
repast of good things to which she invites all:

> Come, eat of my bread,
>> and drink of the wine which I have mingled (9:5).

In a similar manner, Isaias portrays Yahweh inviting his followers to the banquet he has prepared:

> All you who are thirsty,
>> come to the water! . . .
> Heed me, and you shall eat well,
>> you shall delight in rich fare.
> Come to me heedfully,
>> listen that you may have life
>
>> (Is 55:1–3; cf. 25:6; 65:11–13).

Like Yahweh, Wisdom sends out her servants (9:3; cf "my servants the prophets" in Jer 7:25, etc.) to summon all to the banquet. Like the banquet of Yahweh, the feast of Wisdom offers life (9:6, 11) to those who partake of it. But the one who prefers to accept the "stolen water" and "bread gotten secretly" (9:17) in the house of Dame Folly will find himself "in the depths of the nether world" (9:18).

Beneath all this metaphor the author is telling us that his book constitutes Wisdom. All that he has said is merely to entice the reader to the "good life," to get him to live by the collection of proverbs he is presenting. He chose the personification of wisdom in order to express this idea. The interpretation of wisdom in a Christological sense (justifiable in the light of St. Paul), or even in a mariological sense (as is done sometimes in the liturgy), has led to the neglect of the significance which the inspired author himself attributed to the personification. He merely wants to emphasize the direct action of divine wisdom among men, and the personification of divine wisdom is a means to this end.

We have seen the purpose of the author in providing an introduction, and the spirit in which he conceived his task. He is a very intense teacher who offers a lofty concept of wisdom and her function. But he also has the tidy mind of a sage. His introduction is designed to be a well-structured abode for wisdom:

Wisdom has built her house,
She has set up her seven columns (9:1).

What are the seven columns? There have been many answers proposed, for example, that this is a picture of an ordinary well-to-do house or, more fancifully, that these columns derive from the great Etemenanki temple of Babylon. But it seems that only recently have these seven pillars been located with any certainty, and that by the minute and exacting calculations — verbal and stichometric — of Msgr. Patrick W. Skehan of the Catholic University of America. The seven columns are to be identified (and read) thus:

Column 1: 2:1–22, which presents the chapter headings of the columns to follow.

Column 2: 3:1–12 and 25–34; cf. 2:5–8, which enunciates the general topic of column 2: the service of God.

Column 3: 3:13–24 and 4:1–9; cf. 2:9–11, the search for wisdom.

Column 4: 4:10–27 and 5:21–23; cf. 2:12–15, avoidance of evil men and their evil ways.

Column 5: 5:1–20
Column 6: 6:20–21 and
           6:23–7:6   cf. 2:16–19, avoidance of evil
Column 7: 7:7–27   women and their evil ways.

It is recommended that the reader study the introduction in the light of this structure which the author originally gave to it and in the light of the purpose explained above.

Proverbs of Solomon I (10:1–22:16) and II (25:1–29:7)

Astonishment is one of the first reactions registered by the average reader of Proverbs, astonishment at the unflagging optimism in matters of retribution: virtue, with which wisdom is identified, brings reward ("life," "blessings," "joy," "favor," etc.); and vice, which is folly, brings punishment ("death," "rod," "downfall," "trouble"). The Christian reader must be alert to the fact that the retribution is envisioned for this life only. For the wisdom writer, as for Old Testament man, there is no judgment, and hence reward or punishment, after death. There is only Sheol or the nether world, where man ("the shades," Prv 21:16) drags out a bleak existence, as is graphically described in Job 10:21 f. and Coheleth 9:10. As we shall see, apart from some hints in the Psalms and Isaias, knowledge of a blessed future life came only at the end of the Old Testament period with the books of Daniel and Wisdom.

Hence the sages had to work out the problem of retribution, God's just dealing with good and evil men, within the framework of this earthly life. The Jew took a firm stand upon the principle derived from his fathers and enshrined in the Deuteronomist viewpoint of history (Jos, Jgs, Sm, Kgs): God blesses the good, punishes the evil. With stanch faith he reiterates this principle in various forms. Death for the wicked will be sudden, premature, painful, because he must part with his ill-gotten goods. Life for the just will be marked by happiness and prosperity in a full number of years. But it is the writer's faith that speaks, not his experience. He betrays his knowledge of the hard facts of life; he knows the wicked man gains profits, but he calls them "empty" (11:18); sinners are not to be emulated (23:17); even if the just man falls, he will get up again (24:16). Yet he stubbornly glosses over unpleasant facts which contradict his optimism and insists on reward for the virtuous. We cannot call this point of view blind, but is it one-sided, premised on a faith in Yahweh's justice as applied to this life. It is too much to call this a "theory," for it is not developed or defended by any reasoning. It was the response of faith, and it was the best solution the Old Testament man had for a problem which still haunts the human race. It will be easy for the reader to side with the author of Job, who demolishes the traditional point of view of the wisdom writers; but their spirited defense of tradition merits grudging admiration.

As it is, there is a very real truth behind the formulation of this traditional view, specifically in the concept of *life* that is promised to the virtuous. At times it can mean only years, length of life (cf. 10:27); but most often it is a general, all-embracing concept:

> In the path of justice there is life,
> but the abominable way leads to death (12:28).

Other metaphors are employed: tree of life (11:30; 13:12; 15:4), path of life (6:23; 10:17; 15:24), fountain of life (10:11; 13:14; 14:27; 16:22). These are often in contrast to physical death, but they also suggest a fullness that goes behind physical existence:

> Hope deferred makes the heart sick,
> but a wish fulfilled is a tree of life (13:12).

> A path of life is his who heeds admonition,
> but he who disregards reproof goes astray (10:17).

The choice of the metaphor, "tree of life," is surprising when one considers the unfortunate decision in Paradise (Gn 3:5-6, "the tree of knowledge of good and evil"). It suggests that among the sages the knowledge of good and evil, far from being evil, was necessary; their purpose was to instruct in such matters. Knowledge of good and evil was no longer the same thing that it was for the writer of Genesis; it was now wisdom, whose "beginning" is the fear of the Lord (Prv 1:7).

The importance of this vague notion of life is that it is susceptible of development through the rest of the Old Testament and into the New. In the book of Sirach the same concept of wisdom as life, a source of living water, appears:

> The root of wisdom is fear of the Lord;
> her branches are length of days (1:18).

> A wise man's knowledge wells up in a flood,
> and his counsel, like a living spring (21:13).

What is life ultimately? Will it include association with God beyond the earthly span? Eventually it will, and one is reminded of Christ's words, "I am the resurrection and the life" (Jn 11:25).

Thus the very formulation of the traditional view carried within itself the seeds of belief in a blessed immortality.

Several proverbs clearly bear the mark of their origin among the teachers at the royal court; such are those treating of the king:

> The king's lips are an oracle;
>> no judgment he pronounces is false. . . .
> Kings have a horror of wrongdoing,
>> for by righteousness the throne endures.
> The king takes delight in honest lips,
>> and the man who speaks what is right he loves.
> The king's wrath is like messengers of death,
>> but a wise man can pacify it (16:10–14).

There is a healthy respect for the monarchy, both from the religious as well as the practical point of view which is more usually associated with a courtier. Kingship in Israel could never permanently adopt the absolutism which characterized the monarchs in neighboring states. Beneath all the royal dignity was a human:

> Like a stream is the king's heart in the hand of the Lord;
>> where it pleases him, he directs it (21:1).

The practice of bribery and favoritism is never absent from court. There are several observations in Proverbs which might be hastily construed as approval:

> A man's gift clears the way for him,
>> and gains him access to great men (18:16; cf. 19:6).

But the point of the saying is merely to make the youth aware of the workings of the court. Elsewhere, bribery is condemned outright:

> The wicked man accepts a concealed bribe
>> to pervert the course of justice (17:23; cf. 15:27).

The training of a courtier was more universal than we might expect, as indicated by the general content of the two Solomonic collections: duties to God as well as king, personal good habits, social obligations (the poor, etc.), duties to parents, conduct toward one's fellow man, and so forth. Even if the origin of the Proverb literature is the court, it is by no means tied to the world of officialdom. One may even speak of a certain "religious humanism," for the education was directed to the formation of the whole man. We will attempt briefly to illustrate some of these themes.

The fear of the Lord is one of the primary virtues the sage strives to implant in his student. We should be careful not to identify this with servile fear; it is close to humility, to an honest evaluation of one's self before the supreme God. In 22:4 it is bracketed with humility:

> The reward of humility and fear of the Lord
> is riches, honor and life (cf. also 15:33).

And it is also a parallel to kindness and piety:

> By kindness and piety guilt is expiated
> and by the fear of the Lord man avoids evil (16:6).

Hence fear of the Lord represents a total commitment of the person to Yahweh, and the editor of Proverbs had reason to write that it is "the beginning of knowledge" (1:7), "the beginning of wisdom" (9:10).

The Lord is all-knowing and powerful, from whom none can escape:

> The eyes of the Lord are in every place,
> keeping watch on the evil and the good (15:3).

> The nether world and the abyss lie open before the Lord;
> how much more the hearts of men! (15:11; cf. 21:2.)

Even if man has his plans, it is Yahweh who is the supreme cause and agent:

> In his mind a man plans his course,
> but the Lord directs his steps (16:9; cf. 19:21).

> The Lord has made everything for his own ends,
> even the wicked for the evil day (16:4).

This evil day is principally the day of death, since on that day the wicked man must leave behind all that he may have gained by evildoing. There is no implication of judgment and future punishment; the day is simply evil because he is parted from the things in which he found pleasure. On the other hand, one who entrusts his works to the Lord is bound to succeed (16:3).

The Lord's dominion is described more graphically and with greater social implications in 22:2 (cf. 29:13):

> Rich and poor have a common bond:
> the Lord is the maker of them all.

The sympathy of the sage lies with the poor:

> He who shuts his ear to the cry of the poor
> will himself also call and not be heard (21:13; cf. 19:17).

> He who oppresses the poor blasphemes his Maker
> but he who is kind to the needy glorifies him (14:31).

One reason for this sympathy is the correct evaluation of riches. Wealth is consistently put in second place:

> How much better to acquire wisdom than gold!
> To acquire understanding is more desirable than silver
> (16:16; cf. 22:1).

> Better a little with virtue
> than a large income with injustice
> (16:8; cf. 11:4; 15:16, 19:1).

This does not mean that wealth is not a serious consideration for the sage; he aims to make his pupil a success in life, and wealth is part of it. Hence his advice:

> Wealth quickly gotten dwindles away,
> but amassed little by little, it grows (13:11).

> Wealth adds many friends,
> but the friend of the poor man deserts him (19:4).

There is a certain ambivalence in the attitude toward wealth. While it is clearly secondary, it is nevertheless a sign of God's blessing:

> It is the Lord's blessing that brings wealth,
>   and no effort can substitute for it (10:22).

And may one conclude, then, that poverty is a sign of God's displeasure, an indication that God is punishing a man for wrongdoing? Such a conclusion was never widely drawn; it was part of the rigid, doctrinaire criticism which the three friends made concerning Job, but the attitude of the wisdom writers toward the poor is much more understanding and sympathetic.

The sage is particularly vehement in denouncing laziness, which he recognized as a frequent cause of poverty:

> The door turns on its hinges,
>   the sluggard, on his bed! (26:14.)

> The sluggard says, "A lion is outside;
>   in the streets I might be slain" (22:13).

Although the door turns on its hinges, it moves nowhere — so the sluggard, who is ready to grasp at any excuse. He will reap no harvest because he has not sown (20:4); he is like one dining, who will not even lift the food to his mouth (19:24; 26:15), or a hunter who cannot catch his prey (12:27). And his fate?

> A little sleep, a little slumber,
>   a little folding of the arms to rest —
> Then will poverty come upon you like a highwayman,
>   and want like an armed man (24:33 f.).

Strong family discipline is urged again and again. "Spare the rod and spoil the child" is practically derived from such statements as:

> He who spares the rod hates his son,
>   but he who loves him takes care to chastise him (13:24).

> Folly is close to the heart of a child,
>   but the rod of discipline will drive it far from him (22:15).

However, this insistence upon rigid discipline deserves to be balanced by other observations; there was no desire to crush the human spirit:

A man's spirit sustains him in infirmity —
  but a broken spirit who can bear? (18:14.)

Rather, there is a tendency to seek joy and cheer:

A joyful heart is the health of the body,
  but a depressed spirit dries up the bones (17:22).

Every day is miserable for the depressed,
  but a lighthearted man has a continual feast (15:15).

Amen-em-Ope and the Sayings of the Wise (22:17–24:22)

The mention of Amen-em-Ope in Proverbs 22:19 comes as a distinct surprise to most readers of the Old Testament; only the Confraternity of Christian Doctrine (CCD) translation adopts this daring conjectual reading for verse 19. But all who study this book agree that there is some relation between chapters 22–24 and the *Instruction* of Amen-em-Ope, the Egyptian sage. The majority opinion holds that the Hebrew chapters are derived from the Egyptian, not by way of translation, but as a model for thirty sayings. The basic argument turns on more than the fact that the teaching in both is very much the same; what is significant is the organization of both teachings in thirty "sayings" or chapters. We know relatively little about Amen-em-Ope, the son of Ka-nakht. He wrote thirty chapters (or "houses" as he calls them) for his oldest son, who was a priest of the temple of Min at Panapolis. The sayings are more diffuse in style than those of the Hebrew writer; they are preserved for us in a British museum papyrus which purportedly came from Thebes. But the date of the papyrus is uncertain; it is difficult to say more than that it is somewhere within 1000 B.C.–600 B.C.

The Egyptian begins his little treatise: "The beginning of the teachings of life . . . the rules for courtiers to know how to return an answer to him who said it, and to direct a report to one who has sent him [cf. Prv 22:21!]. . . ." The first of the thirty chapters is markedly similar to 22:17–18:

Amen-em-Ope	*Proverbs*
Give thy ears, hear what is said,	Incline your ear, and hear my words,
Give thy heart to understand them.	and apply your heart to my doctrine;
To put them in thy heart is worth while.	For it will be well if you keep them in your bosom (22:17–18a).

The Hebrew style in these chapters is usually structured by couplets. Generally an admonition is given, followed by the reason for it, as exemplified in 22:24 f.:

> Be not friendly with a hotheaded man,
>   nor the companion of a wrathful man,
> Lest you learn his ways,
>   and get yourself into a snare.

These lines can be compared with the advice of the Egyptian:

> Do not associate to thyself the heated man,
> Nor visit him for conversation . . .
> Do not leap to hold to such a one,
> Lest a terror carry thee off.

Ordinarily the "reasons" are not regularly given in Amen-em-Ope's rather diffuse narrative. Both the Hebrew and the Egyptian warn against overestimating wealth; for both it can disappear like a bird:

Amen-em-Ope	*Proverbs*
Cast not thy heart in pursuit of riches . . .	Toil not to gain wealth, cease to be concerned about it;
If riches are brought to thee by robbery,	While your glance flits to it, it is gone!
They will not spend the night with thee . . .	for assuredly it grows wings,
They have made themselves wings like geese	like the eagle that flies toward heaven (23:4 f.).
and are flown away to the heavens.	

Several more examples of the similarity between the "Sayings of the Wise" and the thirty chapters of the Egyptian sage could be given. For details one may refer to the translation of the Egyptian work published in *Ancient Near Eastern Texts* (Princeton University Press, 1950), with the table of comparisons on page 424.* The essential point is that we have here tangible evidence of the high regard in which Egyptian wisdom was held by the Hebrews. The same regard for Arabian or Edomite wisdom will appear in Proverbs 30–31.

The Words of Lamuel (31:1–9) and Agur (30:1–14)

Once more the compiler of Proverbs has included some sayings of a non-Jewish sage. Massa, the home of Lamuel and Agur, seems best identified as a town in northern Arabia, associated with the Ismaelites (cf. Gn 25:14). King Lamuel relates the advice given him by his mother concerning women, wine, and justice. The recommendations are nothing new in view of what is contained in the rest of the book.

Agur's short message is mostly taken up with a commonplace: the inaccessibility of wisdom for man. This is a frequent theme in the wisdom literature (Jb 28; Eccl 7:23–25; Sir 1:1–8). The key affirmation is that wisdom is with God and no one else; man of himself has no real wisdom. Agur emphasizes his lack of intelligence, precisely because he is a sage and knows how little his "wisdom" avails in comparison to God's. The "holy ones" (correcting the text in 30:3), or members of the heavenly court, have knowledge because of their association with Yahweh. It is into this elect circle that man must somehow enter to attain wisdom, but:

> Who has gone up to heaven and come down again —
> Who has cupped the wind in his hands? (30:4.)

Job points out how, although precious metals are to be found somewhere in the world, wisdom — which is more precious than

---

* The translations by John A. Wilson (Egyptian) and Robert H. Pfeiffer (Akkadian) are quoted in this book with the kind permission of the Princeton University Press.

all — is not to be found in the nether world, and is hidden to all creatures:

> The abyss declares, "It is not in me";
>   and the sea says, "I have it not."
> Abaddon and Death say,
>   "Only by rumor have we heard of it" (Jb 28:14, 22).

God alone "knows the way to it" (28:23) and has thrown a hint to man: the fear of the Lord (28:28).

This theme of the inaccessibility of wisdom is balanced by an opposite: Wisdom's overtures to man:

> Those who love me I also love,
>   and those who seek me find me (Prv 8:17).

Such contrast is typical of Old Testament thought, which moves by extremes. This is disconcerting to the Western mind, but nonetheless this polarity of wisdom brings out the complete truth: inaccessible to men, yet offering herself to men.

Before taking leave of the wisdom of Agur, one should note the two things he requests "before I die" in verses 8–9:

> Put falsehood and lying far from me,
>   give me neither poverty nor riches;
> Lest, being full, I deny you,
>   saying, "Who is the Lord?"
> Or, being in want, I steal,
>   and profane the name of my God (30:8 f.).

This is the only statement in the book of Proverbs which looks for the happy mean.

Although 30:15–33 is not part of Agur's testament, we may note it here, calling attention to verses 18–19:

> Three things are too wonderful for me,
>   yes, four I cannot understand;
> The way of an eagle in the air,
>   the way of a serpent upon a rock,
> The way of a ship on the high seas,
>   and the way of a man with a maiden.

The numerical style, frequent in Old Testament poetry (cf. Amos 1:3–2:6), follows the pattern N *plus 1*, with particular emphasis on the addition, or final member. What is singled out for admiration here is the marvelous secret of locomotion of the eagle, serpent, and ship. The eagle goes through the air without falling, the serpent goes over rock without legs, the ship goes through water without sinking. But the greatest mystery is the progress a man makes with a maid — the secret of life and propagation of the human race that is entailed in "the way of a man with a maiden." The author of the book of Wisdom has written a few lines that are at first sight similar to these verses; filled with remorse, the wicked shall speak of their own sad end:

> Like a ship traversing the heaving water,
> > of which, when it has passed, no trace can be found,
> > no path of its keel in the waves.
> Or like a bird flying through the air;
> > no evidence of its course is to be found — (Wis 5:10–11).

The point made here is, of course, different from that of Proverbs 30:18 f. But the comparison of the ship and bird suggests another, even if inaccurate (in the sense that it does not square with the intention of the original author), interpretation of Proverbs 30:18 f. The eagle leaves no trace in the air, nor the serpent on the rock, and the ship cleaves the water; then perhaps sin between a man and a woman is likewise something which can be covered up? This is the interpretation given by the following verse (20), which has therefore every appearance of being an explanatory gloss:

> Such is the way of an adulterous woman:
> > she eats, wipes her mouth,
> > and says, "I have done no wrong" (30:20).

The Ideal Wife (31:10–31)

The ideal of the *mulier fortis* or "valiant woman" of the Roman liturgy (see the Epistle for the Common of Holy Women or Matrons) is properly the ideal of "worthy wife." It is not for bravery or courage that she is celebrated, but for the homely domestic virtues (which demand no small courage). She makes the family clothes, prepares the food, works before dawn, and cares for the poor. But the practical wife is not all activity:

> She opens her mouth in wisdom
> and on her tongue is kindly counsel (31:26).

She is acute enough to be able to judge the value of a field to be bought, or of a garment to be sold. It is no wonder that she is the idol of her own family, that her husband can be among the leaders of the community.

> Charm is deceptive and beauty fleeting;
> the woman who fears the Lord is to be praised (31:30).

This agrees with what we have seen in other collections within this book:

> He who finds a wife finds happiness;
> it is a favor he receives from the Lord
>   (18:22; cf. 12:4; 19:14).

In view of the many diversified sayings about women in the wisdom literature, this emphasis on the ideal wife is more than welcome.

Conclusion

> The intention in the human heart is like water far below
>   the surface,
> but the man of intelligence draws it forth (20:5).

This saying might be applied to the proverbs themselves; many of them are fairly obvious, but others are penetrating observations on the human scene. Because they are highly individualistic, single formulations of experience and observation, they are not assimilated by successive reading. In fact, some readers might claim that reading them is boring. But that depends on how they are read. Each one has to be analyzed, questioned, and compared to the reader's own experience; often a proverb has to be correlated with Hebrew background before it can be understood. If each proverb is challenged by the reader, the reading will be no trial. In the course of teaching the book of Proverbs over several years this writer has not failed to witness the interest and stimulus that the book provides the modern reader. A practical test can be carried out in this way: From each chapter choose two or three proverbs which are judged the most striking — and compare your choices, and the reasons for them, with the selections made by another reader. This ensures a challenging examination of the text, and it helps toward a greater understanding of individual proverbs; one reaches "the water far below the surface."

3. AN APPROACH TO THE PSALMS*

THE title of this chapter is deliberately cautious. The psalms of the Old Testament can be approached from many broad points of view: the literary stylist will analyze the poetry and imagery of these songs; the liturgist will be alert to correspondence with the great themes of the (Christian) liturgy; the theologian will be interested primarily in the religious doctrine contained in these prayers, and so forth. These separate views have their own validity and fruitfulness, but they do not quite catch the genius of the psalms. The approach proposed in this chapter is basically literary and will offer some insight for the litterateur, liturgist, and theologian alike.

Our approach is described by the formidable German term, *Gattungsgeschichte*, employed by a twentieth-century German biblical scholar, Hermann Gunkel, who first worked out its main lines. This means that the *Gattung*, or literary type, of any psalm determines its particular genius, its motifs, its spirit. The psalmists did not compose their works out of the air, so to speak. There were acknowledged literary types which governed the composition: hymns of praise, thanksgiving songs of an individual or a group, lamentations of an individual or a group, etc. The psalmists more or less naturally followed one of these types as they wrote. Particularly helpful in determining the literary type of a given psalm is the recognition of the original life-setting for which it was written. In a sense, this approach is not really new. It has been remarked of Gunkel that "as in the case of Christopher Columbus and the egg, he had to think it out and turn it to advantage." The ancients, too, sought to capture the life-setting, as many of the

---

* All references to the Psalms are according to the Hebrew numbering; those who are accustomed to the Vulgate (Douay-Rheims) numbering should add one unit for most of the Psalms. Thus, Hebrew Ps 23 = Vulgate Ps 22.

titles which they gave to the psalms suggest. Thus, Psalm 34, entitled a "Praise of God, the Protector of the Just," is referred to David, "when he feigned madness before Abimelech, who forced him to depart" (1 Sm 21:13). Thanks to modern archaeological discoveries and an improved knowledge of the *kinds* of literature we are dealing with, we can correct these early efforts to locate individual psalms within their life-setting.

The classification of the psalms which we will propose is not a rigid division based upon a single principle. The types are distinguished mainly according to literary characteristics: style, recurrent motifs, small grammatical indications. But liturgical indications are also important for distinguishing them, e.g., a prayer on the occasion of offering a thanksgiving sacrifice in the temple. A great number of psalms (some would say, all) have their life situation rooted in a liturgical or cultic act. In fact, literary and liturgical factors acted upon each other in the development of the types in ancient Israel. A particular literary type came to be associated with a given cultic situation; certain features of the cult were echoed in the motifs of the type. But prayers cannot always be expected to conform to type, and there are several examples of "deviation." Moreover, it seems wise to introduce other principles of classification. Thus, content is the primary consideration in treating the so-called royal psalms as a unit. Besides, a separate classification serves to point up the significance and uniqueness of the royal psalms. Similarly, another group is classified as wisdom psalms because various aspects of wisdom are discussed (1, 37, 49, 73, 78, 91, 111, 112, 119, 127, 128, 133).

We will explain and exemplify the several literary types to be found in the psalms: hymns, laments, thanksgiving songs, and royal psalms. But the following descriptive analysis will be more meaningful to the reader who has his copy of the psalms at hand.

Hymns

"Hymn" is perhaps an unsatisfactory, although widely used, term for a certain group of psalms. Almost anything that is put to song and utilized in a church is today popularly called a hymn. But in the case of the Old Testament, hymn has the more precise meaning of a song of *praise*. These songs are many and varied, and are found throughout the Old Testament. They exemplify the liveliness and directness of Hebrew poetry at its best; they have movement and appeal, sometimes perhaps too much for the modern taste. The following Psalms are usually classified as hymns: 8, 19:2–7, 29, 33, 65, 68, 96, 98, 100, 103, 104, 105, 111, 113, 114, 117, 135, 136, 139, 144:2–15; 145, 146, 147, 148, 149, 150.

The *introduction* of the hymn is regularly a command or wish to praise the Lord. All kinds of synonyms are used: praise, bless, sing, honor, fear, exult, thank, rejoice; these words set the tone of the poem. They are addressed to an audience, present or absent, that is characterized as the "servants of Yahweh," "children of Sion," "the just," etc. The introduction may be prolonged for several verses:

> Exult, you just, in the Lord;
>   praise from the upright is fitting.
> Give thanks to the Lord on the harp;
>   with the ten-stringed lyre chant his praises.
> Sing to him a new song;
>   pluck the strings skillfully, with shouts of gladness
>
> (33:1–3; cf. 135:1–2).

In a few instances the poet will address himself (103:1; 104:1), but he also calls upon the world:

> Shout joyfully to God, all you on earth,
>   sing praise to the glory of his name;
>   proclaim his glorious praise.
> Say to God, "How tremendous are your deeds!
>   for your great strength your enemies fawn upon you.
> Let all on earth worship and sing praise to you,
>   sing praise to your name!" (66:1–4.)

The *body* of the poem develops the reason for the praise, and this is the real content of the hymn. Over and over again throughout the poem, the reasons for praising Yahweh are stated. The shortest psalm, 117, provides a succinct example:

> Praise the Lord, all you nations;
>> glorify him, all you peoples!
> For steadfast is his kindness toward us,
>> and the fidelity of the Lord endures forever.

To capture the spirit of this little prayer, we have to know from other parts of the Old Testament the meaning of these reasons: the steadfast kindness (*hesed*) and eternal fidelity (*'emet*) which the Lord has shown to Israel throughout history. But here we merely emphasize the literary pattern (praise — because) which holds for all the hymns, no matter how long or developed. The "reasons" provide a rich theology; they include all the various attributes of God, everything that Yahweh meant to Israel.

The jubilant note of the hymns spells out the disinterested worship of Yahweh by the Israelite. In the hymn he rarely requests anything; he simply gives free expression to his enthusiastic praise and worship of God. It is the standpoint of God, not man, that matters. What is this God like? What is it in him which the psalmist calls the people to worship? We would put it abstractly: the attributes of God; but the Hebrew puts in concretely:

> How manifold are your works, O Lord!
>> In wisdom you have wrought them all —
>> the earth is full of your creatures . . .
> They all look to you
>> to give them food in due time.
> When you give it to them, they gather it;
>> when you open your hand, they are filled with good things.
> If you hide your face, they are dismayed;
>> if you take away their breath, they perish
>> and return to their dust (104:24–29).

A favorite theme, not only in hymns, but in other psalm types as well, is creation. The creative act of Yahweh entitles him to praise:

> Let all the earth fear the Lord;
>> let all who dwell in the world revere him.
> For he spoke, and it was made;
>> he commanded, and it stood forth (33:8–9).

The psalmist refers directly to the portrayal in Genesis 1: the creative word of God, "he spoke and it was made." The psalms also give expression to the "mythic" description of this fact; it was a popular rather than theological presentation, and appealed to Hebrew imagination. Yahweh triumphed over *tohu-wavohu*, the original watery chaos, which always threatened the world. Unless he held it in check, even now creation could be destroyed. Chaos was personified in a sea monster, named Rahab or Leviathan in various other biblical texts, whom Yahweh conquered:

> O Lord, God of hosts, who is like you?
>> Mighty are you, O Lord, and your faithfulness surrounds
>> you.
> You rule over the surging of the sea;
>> you still the swelling of its waves.
> You have crushed Rahab with a mortal blow;
>> with your strong arm you have scattered your enemies.
> Yours are the heavens, and yours is the earth;
>> the world and its fullness you have founded (89:9–12).

For the Israelite, however, creation was only one of the great acts of God. Indeed, it is not so much considered in itself as in relation to the "salvation-history" (*Heilsgeschichte*) of the nation, that is, Yahweh's ever-renewed rescue of his People. Even the creation narrative of Genesis 1–2, it has been pointed out, stands in the larger context of God's choice of Abraham and the patriarchs. Creation awakened a practical, religious interest, not scientific curiosity. Yahweh revealed himself to Israel primarily as a savior, and it is these saving acts that are particularly commemorated:

> Come and see the works of God,
>> his tremendous deeds among men.
> He has changed the sea into dry land;
>> through the river they passed on foot;
>> therefore let us rejoice in him (66:5 f.).

Whole psalms are given over to the praise of God for his constant rescue of Israel throughout her history:

> Glory in his holy name;
>   rejoice, O hearts that seek the Lord! . . .
> Recall the wondrous deeds that he has wrought,
>   his portents, and the judgments he has uttered . . .
> When they were few in number,
>   a handful, and strangers there,
> Wandering from nation to nation
>   and from one kingdom to another people,
> He let no man oppress them,
>   and for their sake he rebuked kings (105:3–14; 114, etc.).

The hymns have no formal *conclusion*; they end as simply as they began: by repeating the invitation to praise and sing which was given in the introduction:

> Be glad in the Lord, you just,
>   and give thanks to his holy name (97:12).

> May my mouth speak the praise of the Lord,
>   and may all flesh bless his holy name
>   forever and ever (145:21).

Just as important as the structure of the hymn is its spirit. This can best be characterized as enthusiasm. The Hebrew expression of joy and praise seems almost wild to the Anglo-Saxon. The Hebrew invokes other compatriots, nations of non-Jews, nature itself, to share in his heartfelt praise of God, as exemplified in the great *"Benedicite"* psalms:

> You mountains, and all you hills,
>   you fruit trees and all you cedars;
> You wild beasts and all tame animals,
>   you creeping things and you winged fowl,
> Let the kings of the earth and all peoples,
>   the princes and all the judges of the earth,
> Young men too, and maidens,
>   old men and boys,

Praise the name of the Lord,
    for his name alone is exalted (148:9–13).

Part of this "spirit" that pervades the hymns of the psalter is a certain directness and frankness in speaking of God. The Lord is *real* to the psalmist, for he had an experience of God.

The Hymns of Yahweh's Enthronement

Several psalms are grouped together as hymns of a special type, such as "Songs of Sion" (46, 48, 76, 84, 87, 132), which glorify the Holy City of Jerusalem, and God's designs for it. Some of these do not conform to the literary type of hymn, but all are similar enough to be studied together. Another group, about which a lively discussion has arisen in recent years, comprises the Psalms of Yahweh's Enthronement. There is not even agreement as to the number of hymns to be classified under this rubric; the smallest number is four: 47, 93, 97, 99. For other scholars, who postulate a feast of Yahweh's enthronement as king in ancient Israel, this number can go higher than thirty (e.g., 96, 98, etc.). We will sample the four psalms in order to form a judgment about the Enthronement.

Three of these psalms (93, 97, 99) begin with the ringing cry, *Yahweh malak!* Yahweh is king! This is the theme of these songs: Yahweh's kingship. He is described as awesome and majestic: "throned upon the cherubim" (99:1); "clouds and darkness are round about him" (97:2); "robed and girt about with strength" (93:1). The hymnic character of these pieces is evidenced by the invitation to rejoice and praise (97:1; 99:9; 47:2, 8). The themes that are particularly associated with his kingship are creation and redemption: he has conquered chaos, saved his people:

The floods lift up, O Lord,
    the floods lift up their voice;
    the floods lift up their tumult.
More powerful than the roar of many waters,
    more powerful than the breakers of the sea —
    powerful on high is the Lord (93:3 f.; cf. 95:5; 96:5).

He brings peoples under us;
nations under our feet.
He chooses for us our inheritance,
the glory of Jacob, whom he loves (47:4 f.; cf. 98:2 f.).

The comparison of Yahweh with "other gods" is frequent in these
poems (97:9; 96:4; 95:3); here too, the old Canaanite title for
the titular head of the pantheon, Elyon, "the most High," is the
common epithet of Yahweh (47:3; 97:9). But perhaps the most
remarkable feature is the clear universalism: The nations are
invited to praise him (47:2; 96:7-9; 99:3). The Lord comes (see
the vivid description of a theophany in 97:2-6) to rule and judge
the world (96:13). He is described as having mounted his throne
amid shouts of joy in 47:6; this finds an echo in 2 Samuel 6:15
where the same public demonstration marks the procession and the
installation of the Ark of the Covenant in Jerusalem. The very
cry, "Yahweh is king," is suggestive of the acclamation given to
the new king (Absalom, 2 Sm 15:10; Jehu, 4 Kgs 9:13). Could
it be that these psalms were sung on a like occasion, when Yahweh
("seated" on the Ark) was carried in procession and enthroned in
the Jerusalem temple? Such is the interpretation of the Norwegian
scholar, Sigmund Mowinckel, who has postulated an annual feast
of Yahweh's enthronement, which coincided with the New Year.
Mowinckel's arguments are too detailed to examine here; it is
enough to say that the feast and its rites are postulated and explained by a Babylonian parallel, the New Year Akitu feast in
which Marduk's enthronement was enacted. In both Israel and
Babylon there is a similar pattern: a procession and demonstration,
and similar themes: creation and rule over the world. However,
not a single reference to such a feast is to be found in the rest
of the books of the Old Testament, and many scholars consider
this a decisive reason to reject the interpretation. The only evidence
is the psalms themselves, and this is far from conclusive. The
references to enthronement and procession, it is urged, can be
taken as a mere modus loquendi: The metaphors of human kingship and royal ritual are simply applied to Yahweh, but there is
no feast. However divided be the opinion on the life-setting of

these psalms, all scholars are in agreement that they commemorate Yahweh's kingship over the world; it is important not to lose sight of that fact in appreciating these psalms.

The Psalms of Lament or Complaint

These psalms of lament predominate among the various literary types found in the Psalter. About one third of the psalms are put in this group: 3, 5, 7, 13, 17, 22, 25, 26, 27:7–14; 28, 31, 35, 38, 39, 40:13–18; 42–43; 51, 52, 54, 55, 56, 57:8–12; 59, 61, 63, 64, 69, 70, 71, 86, 88, 102, 109, 130, 140, 141, 142, 143. Closely allied to this classification are the psalms of trust; here the complaint has disappeared and the motif of trust in Yahweh for help dominates: 11, 16, 23, 27, 41, 62, 131. The literary form of supplication or complaint also finds a vivid expression elsewhere in the Old Testament, as in Job (cf. 6:2–7:21; 9:25–10:22; 13:23–14:22; 16:6–17:9; 19:7–20; 23:2–17; 29:1–31:37) and in Jeremias (11:18–20; 15:15–21; 17:12–18; 18:18–23; 20:10–13). The life-setting of these psalms seems to be unmistakable: the psalmist is in dire straits and he cries out to God for help. However, in the case of certain of the psalms (e.g., 22) one has the impression that the reason for the complaint is really past, that God has already answered the psalmist's prayer. We shall return to this characteristic.

The *introduction* is an invocation of the divine name, Yahweh, to which is often joined various epithets, either general, such as "God of hosts" and "God of Israel" (69:7), or specific, such as those that characterize the psalms of trust, "my rock and my redeemer" (19:15). The psalmist invokes Yahweh in a cry for help, as "Save me, O God" (69:2), or merely makes a request for a hearing, "Hear, O God, my voice in my lament" (64:2).

The *body* of the psalm consists in the complaint and the request, either of which may come first, and both of which are repeated frequently throughout the poem.

The *request* consists of imperatives — in general terms, as "hear" (28:2; 17:6), "look" (25:19), "wake up" (7:7; 3:8), and often in specific terms: "heal me" (41:5), "have pity on me" (6:3). It is interesting to note the difference in the request of a penitent sinner:

> If you, O Lord, mark iniquities,
>   Lord, who can stand?
> But with you is forgiveness,
>   that you may be revered (130:3–4).

Here there is no explicit request for forgiveness; the sins are freely admitted and the psalmist relies on the forgiveness that is characteristic of God. On the other hand, the request of a man who considers himself innocent of sin and who asks that he may not die with sinners is to be found in 26:2 ff.:

> Search me, O Lord, and try me;
>   test my soul and my heart.
> For your kindness is before my eyes,
>   and I walk in your truth.
> I stay not with worthless men,
>   nor do I consort with hypocrites.

In the *complaint* the poet pours out his trouble. He tells what happened to him, often giving a vivid description of the affliction from which he is suffering. By and large, this is couched in extreme and even contradictory language (as in Ps 22, where the poet is pursued by wild animals *and* the sword) which in the course of time has become a cliché in this type of literature. One must remember that the Hebrew is not concerned about a literal description, but wants to convey the impressions and feelings that he has. Indeed, the language is sometimes so vague that it is impossible to be sure of the precise nature of his suffering. Thus he will speak of the nether world (oddly enough he uses synonyms most of the time rather than the dread word, Sheol) as the place he is in or approaching. As synonyms he uses for Sheol *grave* or *dust* (30:10), so close to death is he, but he may neglect to specify the cause. A very common cause of his affliction seems to be external sickness, as when his sighing has reduced him to skin and bone (102:6). Or his description may be too vague to pin down, as when he says he is languishing (6:3). But one may question how far these references to sickness are to be pressed. The complaint may be made about several things: absence from Sion (42–43), the shortness of life (39:5–7), man's general misery (71), false accusations (7), the problem of evil, whether individual (73) or communal (83), and, particularly, the enemies of the psalmist.

The most common complaint in the Psalter is enemies, who figure in about thirty psalms. They are described as hunting down the innocent (22:17), or as robbers, spying and murdering (10:8 f.), or as wild animals ready to consume the innocent (7:3). When the psalmist leaves the realm of metaphor, he describes them as looking forward to his death; he fears particularly their tongues; their calumny and insult; and often he quotes their jibes against him (35:21, 25; 64:6). Various theories have been advanced to define more closely this class of evildoers; some have thought they are magicians of a sort who were able to cast a spell, to produce the sickness of which the psalmist so often complains. But frequently there is no mention of sickness, and in the book of Job the same attitude is expressed toward enemies (Jb 16:7 ff.; 19:22, etc.). One is tempted to say that much of the talk about enemies is part of the emotional language in which the poet indulges; because of his dire straits he imagines himself surrounded by enemies, and this situation became part of the language of complaint. On the other hand, this was not always imagination. According to the traditional point of view, a sick man is one who is struck by God, an outcast and deserving of punishment; hence it was easy for his relatives and acquaintances to turn against him, to become his "enemy."

The description of such unmitigated misery is intended to move Yahweh to intervene in the poet's behalf. After all, as the psalmist sees it, Yahweh is in some sense the author and cause of his plight; Yahweh is angry (6:2; 38:2), punishing him for his sins (40:13), or if he is not conscious of personal wrongdoing, he still recognizes God as the author of his affliction. Therefore he must move Yahweh and touch his heart, and here the psalmist shows himself very adroit in persuading God to intervene in his behalf. He adduces several clearly recognizable motives, of which the most important is his trust in Yahweh.

Trust in God is the basic reason why the psalmist even utters his complaint, and it is expressed in various forms:

> Keep me, O God, for in you I take refuge (16:1).

> The Lord is my light and my salvation;
>> whom should I fear?
> The Lord is my life's refuge;
>> of whom should I be afraid? (27:1.)

> O Most High, when I begin to fear,
>> in you will I trust.
>>> In God, in whose promise I glory,
>>> in God I trust without fear;
>>> what can flesh do against me? (56:4–5.)

> My soul waits for the Lord
>> more than sentinels wait for the dawn (130:6).

> I stretch out my hands to you;
>> my soul thirsts for you like parched land (143:6).

Or the poet will encourage himself to trust:

> Why are you so downcast, O my soul?
>> why do you sigh within me?
> Hope in God! For I shall again be thanking him,
>> in the presence of my savior and my God (42:6).

He is particularly anxious to proclaim what Yahweh means to him. Thus, phrases like "my God" (7:2) are not to be dismissed as mere invocations; Yahweh is his God: "his savior" (24:5); "my rock and my fortress" (31:4); "a tower of strength" (61:4).

In a mood that is halfway between trust in God and self-pity, the poet often introduces other special themes that are calculated to move Yahweh. For example, there is the shortness of this life:

> Remember how short my life is;
>> how frail you created all the children of men! (89:48.)

> A short span you have made my days,
>> and my life is as naught before you;
>> only a breath is any human existence (39:6).

Moreover, Yahweh will miss him sorely should he die:

> My eyes have grown dim through affliction;
>> daily I call upon you, O Lord;
>> to you I stretch out my hands.
> Will you work wonders for the dead?
>> will the shades arise to give you thanks?
> Do they declare your kindness in the grave,
>> your faithfulness among those who have perished?
> Are your wonders made known in the darkness,
>> or your justice in the land of oblivion? (88:10–13.)

Since the Hebrew thought that life in Sheol excluded any appeal to God, even any worship of him, this motif is common in the psalms. Yahweh should therefore keep his worshiper alive; let him look to his own interest and save the afflicted; his honor is involved. It may also be that the poet is suffering for the sake of God (69:8).

Yahweh's intervention in Israel's history is another theme. Why can he not intervene in favor of the psalmist?

> In you our fathers trusted;
>> they trusted, and you delivered them.
> To you they cried, and they escaped;
>> in you they trusted, and they were not put to shame
>>>> (22:5–6).

But the psalmists are also aware, by personal experience, of Yahweh's care for them:

> To you I was committed at birth,
>> From my mother's womb you are my God (22:11).

> Who will rise up for me against the wicked?
>> Who will stand by me against the evildoers?
> Were not the Lord my help,
>> I would soon dwell in the silent grave (94:16 f.).

The *conclusion* of the psalm of lamentation is generally marked by a certainty that the prayer has been heard, and often by a vow to offer praise to God. This optimism is a most unusual feature and calls for explanation. The tone of the psalm may lead somewhat naturally to this certainty; the trust which characterized the prayer is now rewarded; the psalmist need no longer request, for Yahweh has heard his prayer. This feeling of certainty is expressed rather mildly in most cases; in Psalm 27:6 one has the impression it has grown quite naturally out of the psalmist's strong faith in God:

> Even now my head is held high
>   above my enemies on every side.
> And I will offer in his tent
>   sacrifices with shouts of gladness;
> I will sing and chant praise to the Lord.

He trusts so completely in Yahweh's justice that he can even urge others to trust in God:

> Cast your care upon the Lord,
>   and he will support you;
>   never will he permit the just man to be disturbed.
> And you, O God, will bring them down
>   into the pit of destruction;
> Men of blood and deceit shall not live out half their days.
>   But I trust in you, O Lord (55:23 f.).

Expressions of this nature are to be found in 3:8; 7:11–18; 26:12; 36:13; 94:22 f.; 130:7 f.; 140:12–14. However, in certain psalms the sudden change to certainty is very marked, as in 56:10–14:

> Then do my enemies turn back,
>   when I call upon you;
>   now I know that God is with me.
>   in God, in whose promise I glory,
>   in God I trust without fear;
>   what can flesh do against me?

Similar striking changes in mood are registered in 6:9–11; 20:7; 57:8–12; 61:6. The Lord has answered and the psalmist praises him for his goodness. Perhaps the most noticeable change occurs in Psalm 22. After an agonizing description of suffering and a desperate plea, the psalmist continues in 22:23–26:

> I will proclaim your name to my brethren;
>   in the midst of the assembly I will praise you:
> "You who fear the Lord, praise him;
>   all you descendants of Jacob, give glory to him;
>   revere him, all you descendants of Israel!
> For he has not spurned or disdained
>   the wretched man in his misery,
> Nor did he turn his face away from him,
>   but when he cried out to him, he heard him."
> So by your gift will I utter praise in the vast assembly;
>   I will fulfill my vows before those who fear him.

What happened at this point? It is as if the psalmist were now serenely offering thanksgiving in the temple.

To explain such violent transitions and, in general, the origin of this certainty, scholars have assumed that the answer was actually given, but has been omitted in the psalm. A priest would have pronounced an oracle from Yahweh that the psalmist would be delivered. This oracle came to be omitted as part of the psalm structure, as laments were used more and more outside the liturgy. Other scholars have concluded instead that these laments, while composed during the distress of which they complain, were delivered in the temple before an assembly some time after the psalmist was delivered. The plea is then merely the recalling of sufferings, a dramatization and reliving of that from which one has finally been freed. Whatever be the correct historical explanation, this feature of certainty deserves careful attention of the reader; it more than compensates for the "complaining" attitude in the psalms.

The National Lamentation

We know of several crises in Israelite history, such as war (Jos 7:6), famine (3 Kgs 8:35 f.) and plague (Jl 1–2), which brought people and leaders together for a major liturgical action. A fast would be proclaimed and an appeal for help sent up to Yahweh. Such is the life-setting of the typical national complaint or lamentation, which includes Psalms 44, 58, 74, 79, 80, 83, 89, 106, 123 (?), 125 (trust), 137. As one might expect, the characteristics of the lamentation of the individual are reproduced here: the appeal to God, with a cry for help; the complaint or cause of the plea; motives of confidence to move Yahweh to intervene; the request; and a certainty that God has heard the prayer, usually with a vow to praise him.

The *introduction* has the usual invocation, but the epithets are more national in character, as 80:2:

> O Shepherd of Israel, hearken,
> O guide of the flock of Joseph!

The *body* explains the dire political situation of the people: 44:10–17; 74:4–11; 79:1–4; 83:3–9. It is typical of the Israelite point of view that the people's distress is couched in moral and religious terms; they face the loss of the temple:

> They set your sanctuary on fire;
> the place where your name abides they have razed and
> profaned.
> They said in their hearts, "Let us destroy them;
> burn all the shrines of God in the land" (74:7 f.).

Slaughter is indiscriminate:

> They have given the corpses of your servants
> as food to the birds of heaven,
> the flesh of your faithful ones to the beasts of the earth.
> They have poured out their blood like water
> round about Jerusalem,
> and there is no one to bury them (79:2–3).

Among the motives used to move Yahweh to act are the questions characteristic of this literary form: Why? How long?

> Why should the nations say,
> "Where is their God?" (79:10.)

> How long, O Lord? Will you hide yourself forever?
> Will your wrath burn like fire? (89:47.)

All the usual methods of "humanizing" Yahweh, of stirring his pity, are employed. He is reminded that it is *his* people, his flock, his vine, his inheritance, that is being destroyed. Both Psalms 74 and 79 speak of the profanation of the temple before describing the sufferings of the people (74:1–2; 79:1–4); therefore let Yahweh look to it. The good old times (44:1–4) are recalled; the frailty of man is stressed (89:48), and sins are confessed (106:6 ff.). Yahweh must intervene "for your name's sake" (79:9), "for your kindness' sake" (44:27). Psalm 125:1–3 contains a strong motive of trust in Yahweh as the Protector of Israel; he will not allow anything to happen to his people:

> They who trust in the Lord are like Mount Sion,
> which is immovable; which forever stands.
> Mountains are round about Jerusalem;
> so the Lord is round about his people,
> both now and forever.
> For the scepter of the wicked shall not remain
> upon the territory of the just,
> Lest the just put forth
> to wickedness their hands.

These motives correspond to those advanced in the psalms of individual complaint; there the psalmist urged that Yahweh keep him alive because he could not praise him in Sheol; here the speakers indicate that Yahweh's glory will be diminished by the victory of the heathen over his people.

The request, as befits the usual passionate tone of the complaint, is usually a strong imperative: "Awake! Why are you asleep, O Lord? Arise!" (44:24.)

> Rouse your power,
> and come to save us (80:3).

The *conclusion* sometimes expresses that remarkable optimism, the certainty of having been heard, and a vow to praise God is expressed:

And we, your people and the sheep of your pasture,
will give thanks to you forever;
through all generations we will declare your praise (79:13).

It is quite clear that the structure of the complaints of the individual and the community are practically the same. The natural
differences are the opposition of "I" to "We," individual to
national distress; furthermore, the descent to Sheol, feared by the
individual, is replaced by the danger of being swallowed up by
heathen nations.

Thanksgiving Psalms of an Individual

There are about a dozen psalms that can be put in this group:
9A (?), 18, 30, 32, 34, 40:2–11; 41, 66 (complex: community,
vv. 8–12; individual, vv. 13–20), 116, 118, 138. The life-setting
to which these psalms correspond is generally considered to be the
cultic thank-offering; some of them have clear references to such
offerings (e.g., 66:13 ff.; 107:22 ff.). But one may well question
whether this type of psalm *must* have a cultic origin. Any saving
intervention of Yahweh was enough to call forth praise of him,
the acknowledgment of his deed, quite apart from a liturgical
celebration.

The *introduction* to these psalms is the same as that of the
hymns of praise:

I will give thanks to you, O Lord, with all my heart;
I will declare all your wondrous deeds (9:2).

Again, like the hymns, it is often expanded for several verses,
containing words like "thank," "praise," which set the tone for
the entire psalm:

I will bless the Lord at all times;
His praise shall be ever in my mouth.
Let my soul glory in the Lord;
the lowly will hear me and be glad.
Glorify the Lord with me,
let us together extol his name (34:2–4).

As against the hymns, where the introduction is usually crowded
with imperatives, there is usually a volitive form, "I will give
thanks to you, O Lord" (138:1; cf. 9:2).

The *body* is characterized by two important features: the story
of the person who is giving thanks, and the acknowledgment of
Yahweh as the rescuer. Thus, psalm 40 even begins with the
story of what happened.

> I have waited, waited for the Lord,
>   and he stooped toward me and heard my cry.
> He drew me out of the pit of destruction,
>   out of the mud of the swamp;
> He set my feet upon a crag;
>   he made firm my steps (40:2–3).

Usually there are three elements to the experience which the
poet relates. He will give an account of the distress he was in,
relate how he called upon Yahweh, and mention the rescue:

> I will extol you, O Lord, for you drew me clear
>   and did not let my enemies rejoice over me.
> O Lord, my God,
>   I cried out to you and you healed me.
> O Lord, you brought me up from the nether world;
>   you preserved me from among those going down into the
>   pit (30:2–4).

Just as in the body of the hymn, the reason for praise follows, so
here the reason for the thanksgiving follows: an account of the
distress the psalmist was in, his calling upon Yahweh, and the
rescue. The description of the danger is very similar to the language used in the psalms of lamentation described above. In fact,
the two situations correspond: one asks to be delivered from
distress which he describes; the other acknowledges God for having delivered him from such distress. Hence, as in the description
of the complaints, one gets the impression that it is a matter of
life and death: sickness, capture, war, the nether world, and
enemies. It is a stereotyped language which tells us how the
psalmist feels, but does not tell us exactly what he is suffering

from. Although the story of Job tells us what happened to him, one would never realize it from such descriptions as given in Job 16:7–17. The same holds for the psalmist; he is encompassed by "cords of death," "the snares of the nether world" (116:3); his enemies "whisper together against" him (41:8); he has been raised up "from the gates of death" (9:14).

The second important element, the acknowledgment of Yahweh as the rescuer, is usually directed to an audience, whether present or merely imagined. The psalmist urges them to follow his example of trust in the Lord, to learn to trust in him:

> Taste and see how good the Lord is;
>> happy the man who takes refuge in him.
> Fear the Lord, you his holy ones,
>> for nought is lacking to those who fear him (34:9–10).

> Happy is he who has regard for the lowly and the poor;
>> in the day of misfortune the Lord will deliver him.
> The Lord will keep and preserve him;
>> he will make him happy on the earth,
>> and not give him over to the will of his enemies.
> The Lord will help him on his sickbed,
>> he will take away all his ailment when he is ill (41:2–4).

To this is sometimes joined an announcement of a thanksgiving offering, as in 66:13–16:

> I will bring holocausts to your house;
>> to you I will fulfill the vows
> Which my lips uttered
>> and my words promised in my distress.
> Holocausts of fatlings I will offer you,
>> with burnt offerings of rams;
>> I will sacrifice oxen and goats.
> Hear now, all you who fear God, while I declare
>> what he has done for me.

It is obvious that a prayer like this is intended to accompany the sacrifice; but the only other clear reference to sacrifice in these thanksgiving psalms is 116:17–19. There are other cultic references, such as the cup of salvation in 116:13, the procession indictated in 118:19–21, the rejoicing at the gates in 9:15, the assembly in 22:23–27 (although Ps 22 is more correctly classified as a lament, rather than a thanksgiving psalm), the temple in 138:2. At any rate, a certain contact between the psalmist and his audience is often expressed; they are to share his joy over his rescue.

If this type of psalm can be said to have a characteristic *ending*, again like the hymn it returns to the beginning:

> Therefore will I proclaim you, O Lord, among the nations,
>   and I will sing praise to your name,
> You who gave great victories to your king
>   and showed kindness to your anointed,
>   to David and his posterity forever
>
> （18:50 f.; cf. 30:13; 40:11; 118:29）.

Finally, we may take brief notice of the collective Thanksgiving Psalms. There is no agreement on their number except that they are relatively rare; Psalms 124 and 129 are the clearest examples and more or less reflect the structure noted above for the thanksgiving psalms of the individual. Psalm 66:5–12 thanks God for having delivered the nation; Psalm 67 thanks him for an abundant harvest but also ends with a request. There are several "victory songs" in the Old Testament which may be classified here: Judges 5 (the song of Deborah); Judith 16 (her victory over Holofernes); cf. Psalms 118:15 f. and 149.

Royal Psalms

The psalms which expressly refer to the king (2, 18, 20, 21, 45, 72, 101, 110, 144:1–11; cf. 89:20–39; 132) do not, properly speaking, form a literary type. They are grouped together because of their content. Although from a literary point of view these psalms are varied, they receive a deeper unity when they are related to their original life-setting: the royal court. They are anchored in particular events of royal life, such as the accession to the throne (e.g., 2, 72), marriage (45), war (18), etc.

It is difficult to overrate the importance of the kingship in Israel. The institution of royalty was a radical change from the days of the charismatic leaders whom Yahweh accompanied into battle. Israel became a state like its neighbors, and a whole world of courtly ceremonial grew up, considerably influenced by the practices of other nations, particularly Egypt. The main events in the life of the court could not pass without an official celebration which assumed a religious as well as an institutional character. For example, the accession to the throne was a double ceremony. In the temple the king was crowned and "legitimized" as the ruler who will serve God and nation (cf. 4 Kgs 11). Then in his palace he ascended the throne and officially announced his royalty (as one may judge from Ps 2) amid the joyous acclamation of his subjects (3 Kgs 1:40). The king became Yahweh's adopted son (2:7) and a world of protocol developed around him. But Israel had little or no antecedent for this; in fact, even with royalty there are evidences that a strong tribal spirit remained, and more than once rebellion was touched off with the cry, "To your tents, O Israel" (2 Sm 20:1; 3 Kgs 12:16). Yet royal protocol had to be established, and for this Israel went to its older neighbors, Egypt and Assyria. Scholars have long pointed out the many parallels in words and ideas between what they call "court style" (the manner of addressing the king) in Israel and the other nations. But this must be understood properly. It would be a caricature, as well as historically insensitive, to think that Israel simply took over the court style of its neighbors. After all, there was no comparison between the stature of the small Israelite state and the world empires. How could an idea of world rule (which we find in Ps 72:8-11) be a genuine expression of Hebrew court style? The answer lies in the oracle of Nathan, the solemn divine promise, in 2 Sm 7. To David's desire to build for God a house or temple Yahweh replied with the assurance that he would build a "house" for David, that the Davidic dynasty would reign forever (2 Sm 7:15 f.; cf. Ps 89). This eternal guaranty of the Davidic line forged a continuity and permanence on the Judean throne that the northern kingdom, with its rapid succession of dynasties, never

achieved. But, more important, it anchored the messianic hope
in the Davidic dynasty. The reigning king came to be viewed in
the light of the messianic dignity with which his line was in-
vested. Therefore, there could be no exaggeration of his glory and
his power which Yahweh secured for him. The courtly style assimilated from the great empires is to be understood in this light.
It provided the relatively new kingdom of Israel with an apt means
to express the meaning and function of its king.

We have just spoken of messianism; in reference to the psalms
under discussion, it may be specified as royal messianism. By this
we mean the characteristic enjoyed by the kings of Jerusalem as
the fulfillment of the divine promise to David. This promise was
to become more and more personalized in later times into the "one
who was to come." The reigning king was the bearer and symbol
of promises made to David (2 Sm 7); he belonged to a dynasty
with which God had made an eternal covenant. Hence there is
no real exaggeration in the psalms written about him; he is a
child of destiny through whom God will eventually achieve his
kingdom. The achievement or fulfillment, which is obviously
not a mathematical verification of the psalms, came in the kingship
of Christ, the Son of David.

Psalm 2 was probably composed to commemorate the accession
to the Jerusalem throne of some descendant of David. It proclaims
the king as the (adopted) son of Yahweh:

> The Lord said to me, "You are my son;
>   this day I have begotten you."

Yahweh merely laughs at the rebellion of the nations (the cus-
tomary revolt in the Near East when a new king is to take over).
He has given his son "the nations for an inheritance." Nothing can
shake the eternal dynasty of David which has been established on
Sion.

Psalms 18 and 21 are prayers of thanksgiving for the king;
Psalms 20 and perhaps 144:1–11 are pleas for the king's safety
and victory. Psalm 101 is the model which the king takes for his
rule, a sort of "mirror of princes." Psalm 45 celebrates the mar-

riage of the king (who is looked upon as an *elohim*-being, in some way supernatural, 45:7) with a royal princess. Psalm 72 is a prayer for the king, probably at his accession or its anniversary, which expresses all manner of good wishes for him: justice, life, prosperity, world-wide rule. Psalm 110, if we adopt the more or less traditional translation of a very uncertain verse, reflects the same adoptive sonship proclaimed in Psalm 2:

> Yours is princely power in the day of your birth, in holy
> splendor;
> before the day star, like the dew, I have begotten you
> (110:3).

However, even if we can never be certain of the reading of this verse, it is clear that 110:1 associates the king intimately with Yahweh, "sit at my right hand."

The king is a "priest forever, according to the order of Melchisedec" (110:4). Throughout the ancient Near East the king is sacred and priestly. David himself feared to lay hand on the Lord's "Anointed," Saul (1 Sm 24:6; 26:9 ff.). However, the priesthood of the king in Israel is rather played down, and the priestly functions come to be assigned to the descendants of Aaron. But in this psalm appears the desire to "regularize" the priesthood of the Davidic descendant in the new capital of Jerusalem. It will be recalled that David first conquered this city from the Jebusites; naturally many of them remained in the capital. To assure them that the Davidic king is also their legitimate priest, the psalmist proclaims that the king is priest on the same terms as their Melchisedec, the old king of Salem, who was a priest of "El Elyon," the most High God (Gn 14:18). Such is the historical meaning of the traditional phrase, *"secundum ordinem Melchisedech."*

Conclusion

It is worth emphasizing what we said above: The fundamental approach to the psalter should be through the various literary types which we have been describing. Only in this way can we ask each psalm the appropriate questions: What is its origin and purpose? What is the author attempting to say? We should ask these questions of all biblical literature, but particularly of the psalms. Because they are intensely personal and religious, their distinctive differences, their "personality" so to speak, can escape us. Then, too, they span some seven centuries of Israel's life and so portray a rich variety of mood, belief, and aspiration. The literary types help us to control such diverse poems.

As for understanding and relishing the content of the Psalter, we may conclude with two observations. First, anyone who has an experience of God, and therefore with prayer, finds himself at home with these inspired songs. Not all of them are equally attractive, but one cannot expect otherwise. Everyone has, or should have, his favorite psalms. These will speak to the human heart beyond all barriers of culture, language, and education. Second, it is also true that a greater understanding of the psalms, a deeper penetration of their meaning, comes from reading them in the light of the rest of the Old Testament ideas and beliefs. One should not be satisfied with a merely personal or self-inspired use of these prayers. They had a meaning for the inspired author, and we should attempt to capture that meaning with its various nuances. To this end, a knowledge of the rest of the so-called Sapiential Books with which we are dealing in this volume will be of real help. Thus, the problem of retribution, God's manner of dealing with men, messianism, etc. — all of these come into play in the psalms themselves. Similarly, the great themes of the historical and prophetical books find an echo in these poems. To read the psalter is to read a cross section of the Old Testament, but understanding the psalms also presupposes a knowledge of the rest of the inspired books.

4. A MAN NAMED JOB

With most books it is generally fatal to read the first couple of chapters and then skip to the end. But for the book of Job such a method may be recommended. It lets us in behind the scenes, so to speak, for it gives us the original folk tale which the author took as the framework of his story; it is within this framework that he writes, adjusting himself to its limitations. Moreover, it is well to understand at the outset that the author is not describing a concrete historical event.

Prologue (1:1–2:13) and Epilogue (42:7–17)

The man Job was an historical character whom the Israelites envisioned as belonging to the patriarchal era (*ca.* 1800). Hence he is described in a manner reminiscent of Abraham, with flock, camels, and great possessions. As patriarch he is priest of his family (1:5). His fabled reputation for justice and integrity was well known in the ancient world, for Ezechiel (14:14, 20) brackets him with the biblical Noe and the Canaanite Danel, who has been generally identified with a just hero in Ugaritic literature. Indeed, it would appear from his origins that the story of Job has entered Jewish tradition from abroad. Both he and his three friends came from Arabia which was reputed for its sages and their wisdom (cf. 3 Kgs 10:1 ff.; Jer 49:7; Bar 3:22–23; Abd 8). Job's story was a simple one; despite great personal suffering and misfortune sustained by a test of his virtue, this just man remained faithful to God. As the biblical author has him say: "The Lord gave and the Lord has taken away; blessed be the name of the Lord" (1:21). To reward his fidelity God gave to Job twice as much as he had before his trial. This folk tale is a concrete formulation of the traditional theory of retribution: God rewards the just and punishes the evil. Even if Job suffered, he is to be rewarded double. The proverb writer accounted for such anomalous suffering:

> For whom the Lord loves he reproves,
> and he chastises the son he favors (Prv 3:12).

In the light of the theory, suffering and misfortune are exceptional for the just man; hence Job's final lot is twice blest.

The term "Satan," or Adversary, should not mislead the Christian reader; this character is a faithful "son of God" whose function is to patrol the earth (1:7; 2:2), presumably fulfilling his duty as a member of the heavenly court. From the point of view of God's interests, he is merely solicitous for the honor of his master. Job is God-fearing? Satan's advice would be: Test him. He is not hostile to Job, but he does not think that Job is as faithful as he seems to be — it is easy for Job to be loyal when he enjoys all the prosperity given him by God. It is only in later revelation that there emerges the Satan whom we know to be the devil, and hostile to God and man. The stilted, artificial conversation between God and Satan which is twice given in full detail is in itself an indication that the author is not describing an historical event. Like his predecessors, he could never conceive of God in splendid isolation: God, like human kings, has a court composed of superior beings called "sons of God" or "holy ones" (1:6; 2:1; 38:7; see also Gn 6:1-4; Ps 82:1, 6; 29:1, etc.). We are in no position to say exactly what these beings meant to the author, except that they, like Satan, apparently served Yahweh.

How is one to judge the test and Job's magnificent submission? Is this merely the machinery or framework for the cycle of the speeches or did the author intend to make a point in the person of Job in chapters 1-2? Some scholars think that he wanted to give an example of *disinterested piety*. According to this interpretation, the author desired to show that unmerited suffering is due to God's trust in man; God honors man by giving him an opportunity to vindicate his trust in him. Somehow it is difficult to admit all this as part of the author's intention. It may be granted that he recognizes no single solution to the problem of suffering. But did he take the device of Satan and the test as seriously as this interpretation would imply? In the cycle of speeches the author betrays a highly refined notion of the divinity. His God is not one to be subject to doubts about the fidelity of his servants or to allow himself to be put on the spot by a challenge from one of the members of his court. We would submit that the author is not serious about the motivation given to God by Satan. Rather, the primitive notion of Satan's testing of Job is merely the necessary machinery for the poem. It was essential to his point that Job suffer without reason; the testing gave the reader a behind-the-scenes view, so as to understand Job's claims in the dialogue. The very fact that in the epilogue the *reason* (God's "wager" with Satan) is not revealed is a good indication that the testing motive is not to be taken seriously; it is merely part of the machinery to set up the situation. Hence we would conclude that the author does not have a subsidiary motif of "Job the patient sufferer" in the prologue; he simply chose this story to work with. Although Job's story may have originally illustrated the thesis of disinterested piety, it was a neat foil for the author, because it provided a good example of the mechanical *quid pro quo* interpretation of retribution.

In its present form, the epilogue, which consists of 42:7-17, betrays the fact that it belonged to the prologue as part of the original folk tale, in that it approves Job's words as against the Three. This verdict of approval was doubtless applicable to the original tale (cc. 1-2), but it is too sweeping for the cycle of speeches composed by the author of Job (cc. 3-41). In the dialogue with Yahweh Job is utterly humbled and admits that:

> Though I have spoken once. I will not do so again;
> though twice, I will do so no more (40:5).

> Therefore I disown what I have said,
> and repent in dust and ashes (42:6).

Therefore it was not of chapters 3-41 that the verdict in 42:7 f.

speaks: ". . . for you have not spoken rightly of me, as has my servant Job." The original tale must have contained a different dialogue to which 42:7 gives approval. The author simply retained the ending since it was favorable to Job, his protagonist. The reward follows: double for all he had lost, and a life that is twice the biblical span (70 years).

Objection has been raised against this ending as contradicting the author's message. However, it should be granted that the author was simply limited by the original form of the material he was working with. This material demanded a solution; Job cannot be left in Satan's power after passing the test; he must be delivered and rewarded. Rather, may we not detect irony in the author's choice of such an ending for a work that would be a refutation of the traditional theory of retribution?

The Dialogue of Job and His Friends (3–31)

There are three cycles of speeches, as Job alternates with each of the three Friends, but the third cycle has broken down with the disappearance of Sophar, due to textual corruption. We will offer a possible and tentative restoration of these chapters for the convenience of the reader, with the warning that no truly satisfactory sequence has as yet been worked out:

22 – Eliphaz
23, 24 – Job
25:1–6 – Baldad
27:2–6 – Job
27:7–21 – Sophar
26, 28 – Job

The dialogue is rambling and disconcerting, according to our Western manner of logical discussion. Only rarely does a speaker reply specifically to a point raised by his opponent. Each man takes up the argument almost as if his opponent had said nothing. However, the total effect is clear: all the arguments *pro* and *con* find

Have you eyes of flesh?
  Do you see as man sees?
Are your days as the days of a mortal,
  and are your years as a man's lifetime,
That you seek for guilt in me
  and search after my sins,
Even though you know that I am not wicked
  and that none can deliver me out of your hand?
Your hands have formed me and fashioned me;
  will you then turn and destroy me?
Oh, remember that you fashioned me from clay!
  Will you then bring me down to dust again? (10:4–9.)

The thought of death and the desire for it are frequently expressed by Job. It is remarkable that the thought of suicide never asserts itself; the fact is, he loves life and suicide is foreign to his countrymen, except for a very few, as Achitophel and Judas. But his preoccupation with death, which is customarily introduced at the end of his replies, leads him to describe Sheol, or the nether world, at some length. It is the great leveler where all go, kings and servants (3:13–26), the land where "darkness" is the only light (10:22), where corruption and maggots are one's family (17:14). At one point he wishes that God would hide him there:

Oh, that you would hide me in the nether world
  and keep me sheltered till your wrath is past;
  would fix a time for me, and then remember me!
When a man has died, were he to live again,
  all the days of my drudgery I would wait,
  until my relief should come (14:13–14).

This desire is unusual; he wants an "apparent death," and he makes the supposition which he knows is impossible: "were he to live again," Job would wait in Sheol for liberation. At least the thought and desire of returning from death crossed his mind. Some scholars have judged that Job actually proclaimed the resurrection of the body in the famous passage of 19:25 ff. Unquestionably St. Jerome's Vulgate translation contains this affirmation. But neither the Hebrew text nor the ancient versions warrant this interpretation:

> But as for me, I know that my Vindicator lives,
>   and that he will at last stand forth upon the dust
> Whom I myself shall see, and not another —
>   and from my flesh I shall see God;
>   my inmost being is consumed with longing (19:25–27).

The obscurity of these lines (and this is one of the most textually uncertain passages in the Old Testament) should not hide the fact that this passage is a high point in the dialogue. Despite the accusations made against God, Job does not cease to trust in him. Here he makes a tremendous act of faith in God as his Vindicator (*go'el*). God is on Job's side, despite appearances. This is an act of faith in God wherein he expresses his unwillingness to set God down as unjust. The logic of his situation demands that he trust God to right the wrong. It is impossible to determine the time and manner of the event. We have already seen expressed the impossible desire, "were a man to live again" (14:14), but there is no indication that this vision of his Vindicator is to be placed after death. Even if he conceived of a resurrection of the body, he does not see it as a solution to his problem.

We have already noted Chapter 28 while discussing Proverbs above. The point of the chapter is that while precious metals can be found, even though they are secreted in the earth, Wisdom, most precious of all, is not to be found — except in God. Some scholars have interpreted this section as a later insertion by the author, or even as an addition by a later writer. It is somewhat out of character with Job's usual querulous statements. Yet its conclusion is not without pertinence to Job himself:

> The fear of the Lord is wisdom
>   and avoiding evil is understanding (28:28).

This indicates that Job has wisdom, for it is a clear reference to 1:8 and 2:3 where Job is described as "fearing God and avoiding evil."

Job's final plea (29–31) is an *apologia* which terminates the cycle of discourses. He ceases from any further discussion with the Friends, addressing not a word to them, although quite conscious of their presence. He begins by recalling his former prosperity, when God watched over him. With delicate feeling he evokes those days of happiness and service, when he was "eyes to the blind, and feet to the lame" (29:15). Now all this has disappeared in his present affliction (30:1 ff.), when his "harp is turned to mourning" and his "reed pipe to sounds of weeping" (30:31). Eliphaz had listed Job's sins (22:6 ff.); now in Chapter 31 Job defends his innocence in a series of vivid imprecations: if he has committed any crime — impurity, lying, injustice — may he be punished. This is his last plea:

> Oh, that I had one to hear my case,
>   and that my accuser would write out his indictment!
> Surely, I should wear it on my shoulder
>   or put it on me like a diadem;
> Of all my steps I should give him an account;
>   like a prince I should present myself before him.
> This is my final plea; let the Almighty answer me!
>
> (31:35–37.)

This proud challenge would be judged as blasphemy in the mouth of anyone else. One may recall the particularly bitter passage of 9:22–24:

> It is all one! therefore I say:
>   Both the innocent and the wicked he destroys.
> When the scourge slays suddenly,
>   he laughs at the despair of the innocent.
> The earth is given into the hands of the wicked;
>   he covers the faces of its judges.
> If it is not he, who then is it?

Or again, 23:12–14:

> From the commands of his lips I have not departed;
>   the words of his mouth I have treasured in my heart.

But he has decided, and who can say him nay?
What he desires, that he does.
For he will carry out what is appointed for me;
and many such things may yet be in his mind.

Job's belief in God's supremacy and primary causality in all things permitted only the conclusion that God is responsible. Man's innocence is not the deciding factor. Not only is Job puzzled by the arbitrary, mysterious manner of God's dealing with man; he accuses him of injustice, of hounding man and being as petty as a man. Surely then Job cannot be acquitted of blasphemy? One must look to the intention of the author: he deliberately paints a realistic picture for artistic as well as religious reasons. This is a picture taken from life, and a Hebrew who denied the traditional theory would only too often "blaspheme"; what other course did he have? God's justice had to be expressed in this life. But this feature is balanced by two others: Job's retraction (42:5), to which we shall return, and the magnificent faith and trust which shines through his daring statements. The marvel of it all is that he does not despair. If only he could meet God, confront him directly, his problem would be resolved. This desire is expressed several times (13:15; 14:13 f.; 16:19; 19:25 ff.; 23:3), although he fears this encounter (9:16 ff., 32 ff.). It is finally granted in the last scene of the dialogue (38–42), but it is not the victory Job looked forward to.

Eliu (32–37)

In the Old Testament there is no lack of young men who, characteristically, wave aside the graybeards in an effort to have a job done rightly. David knew better than Saul, Joab than Abner, Giezi than Eliseus. Eliu knows better than the Three. With the fire of youth, he interrupts the dialogue, utterly dissatisfied with the success Job has had against the friends; Job is wrong because he thinks himself to be in the right rather than God; the Three are at fault because of their pitiable defense of God (32:2–3). Impatient and impulsive, he boasts of the superior wisdom he is to impart. In the thirty-third chapter he challenges Job; his language is bombastic, but his role is meant to be a serious one. He scores the presumption of Job; how could he claim to be innocent (33:8–11)? God is greater than man! This does not mean God is indifferent. No, he speaks to man by visions, by suffering itself; when man admits his guilt he is restored by the Almighty. To the Three (34:2 ff.) Eliu professes to know how Job is to be answered. Job claimed that man's innocence avails nothing in God's eyes. This is impossible; as creator, he watches over all things. Being almighty, he need not fear, and will show no partiality; his omniscience allows no evil to go unnoticed. By his impious statements Job has added rebellion to his sins. Did Job not say (35:2 ff.) that it mattered not in God's eyes if he sinned, that this did not touch God? It is true that one's sin or virtue does not touch God, but it afflicts mankind. When humans cry out, it is only their pride which will keep God from intervening (35:12). Eliu passes on to explain why God afflicts men. The basic principle is his justice to both the good and bad (36:5–8). The wicked he punishes in order to turn them from their pride, that he may reward them with happiness; if they do not hearken to him, they perish justly.

> But he saves the unfortunate through their affliction,
>   and instructs them through distress (36:15).

Eliu then launches into a glorious hymn in praise of God's Might and Wisdom (36:22–37:13). He ranges through the phenomena of nature: rain, clouds, thunder (God's "voice") and lightning, rain, snow. Let Job contemplate these things and understand:

> The Almighty! we cannot discover him,
>   pre-eminent in power and judgment;
>   his great justice owes no one an accounting.
> Therefore men revere him,
>   though none can see him, however wise their hearts
>   (37:23–24).

For all the importance Eliu attributes to himself and his words, he merely repeats what his friends have said, and really sheds little light on the problem. But perhaps his role can be appreciated in the light of what Yahweh is going to say; he sets the stage for the divine encounter. But it is too much to say that he disposes Job to accept the decisions of Yahweh; Job never answers him! He has not quite the same grist as the Three; he does not belabor the fact (although he believes it) that Job's affliction is a punishment for sin. More supple than his elders, he can see a medicinal character (33:15–29; 36:15), an educative value, in Job's trial, and he seems anxious to correct a proud tendency in Job to set himself up as God. However, the sudden introduction of Eliu, the absence of any reference to him in the prologue or, especially, in the epilogue, his failure to say anything more telling than what the Friends have said — all these arguments have been advanced as proof that he is a later addition to the book. It is not easy to decide, because Eliu's function remains unclear, even as a later addition.

Yahweh (38–42)

As with most of the theophanies in the Old Testament, so here Yahweh appears in a storm. Has Job questioned God? God challenges him: "Gird your loins now like a man!" In a series of "if you know," "can you do," "who can do," questions, he overwhelms Job. These questions ask him ironically if he would be like God — so far has his attack on God's justice led him. Job is to ponder the wisdom of God in the creation and ruling of the world. There follows a description of the creation and operation of the heavens, the earth, the waters, light, the Abyss, Sheol, snow, lightning, flood and rain, and the animal world (cc. 38–39). This magnificent poetry is pointed at Job: "Where were you when I founded the earth?" Job is utterly confused, "I put my hand over my mouth. . . ." Yahweh begins again (40:6 ff.), emphasizing divine omnipotence. There is the famous and vivid description of Behemoth and Leviathan; while man is unable to cope with them, God controls them. Job admits defeat, humbling himself before the mysterious designs of Providence:

I have dealt with great things that I do not understand;
  things too wonderful for me, which I cannot know.
I had heard of you by word of mouth,
  but now my eye has seen you.
Therefore I disown what I have said,
  and repent in dust and ashes (42:3–6).

This is not an admission that the Friends were right after all;
but Job realizes he has gone too far in questioning God. Hearsay
has been replaced by *vision* of God. All his previous experience of
God is as nothing compared with this divine encounter. This is
the answer Job receives: Man must experience God and be brought
to his knees before he "understands" the problem of injustice and
suffering. Really, Yahweh does not say more than what Job could
have said himself (cf. 9:5 ff. and 12:7 ff.). The answer lies less
in what he says than in Job's experience of God and surrender to
him. There is no way of adequately translating this into rational
argument. As we might expect from an Old Testament writer,
the problem is solved in an existential manner. Job can somehow
resolve his doubts and find the reply to his earlier accusations
in this direct encounter with his God. Yet we may say that the
author has communicated something of this experience in the
magnificent speeches of Yahweh. They betray exactly who Yahweh
is, while they represent the impression that the theophany has
made upon Job. As we read chapters 38 to 42, we realize that
man cannot judge God because the scope of the divine activity
is so extremely broad, the whole of creation. Hence the justice of
God transcends man, and no justification can be demanded of it.
If God exercises his providential care over the various creatures
instanced in these chapters, the inference is that he must care for
man all the more. There is far more mystery in God's dealings with
the world than either the traditionalists or Job allow. Only faith
and humility permit man to "see" this.

It is difficult to pinpoint the intention of the author in writing
this book. All would agree that he opposes the traditional theory
in the mechanical form advanced by the three Friends. Suffering
and sin are not correlative. But it may be questioned if he would

repudiate the tradition entirely. He shows up its limitations, but he does not replace it with a new theory. Where it breaks down in individual cases, he would say, we have evidence of the different levels at which God's justice operates. The appeasement of one who suffers unjustly is to be found in the experience of God — a religious, existential answer to the problem of suffering. Even in the New Testament we have not gone substantially beyond Job. The knowledge of a blessed immortality in the next life assuages suffering in this world, but it does not solve the problem of God's justice. The only real progress is the Cross — itself a mystery, which is, as it were, a continuation of Job's sufferings.

5. THE SONG OF LOVE

I T IS hardly an exaggeration to say that the average Bible reader
remains somewhat indifferent to the Canticle of Canticles, or
Song of Songs, as it is also called. There are so many other
biblical books that seem more important and more pertinent, and
certainly less mysterious. And just what is the religious content of
this unusual work, in which the name of God is not mentioned?
Yet the considered judgment of the Jews themselves ranked this
small poem highly. To the famous Rabbi of the second century
A.D., the learned Akiba, is attributed the statement: "The world
itself is not worth the day on which this book was given to Israel."
We shall try to appreciate the truth of his words.

A Song

First of all, the Canticle is a song, or more exactly, a composition of several songs. It is well to recall this, because we are in-
clined to look upon it as a book to be read and analyzed, like the
book of Ruth. But the title, "Canticle of Canticles," which is the
Hebrew style of expressing the superlative (the best Canticle),
is quite correct; we are dealing with song(s). Originally, before
the Canticle was received into the canon of the sacred books,
parts of it were undoubtedly sung. This is not unusual among the
books of the Old Testament. As we have seen, the book of Psalms
contains many hymns which were sung, whether by an individual
or a group. Indeed, we observed that an analysis of a hymn often
enabled us to arrive at its life-setting, that is, the actual occasion
on which it was sung. Can we do the same for the Canticle of
Canticles? Is there any indication of the circumstances in which
this poem was sung? Père Jean-Paul Audet, O.P., in a penetrating
study, has pointed out that Jeremias and Osee suggest the answer.

A Wedding Song

No less than four times (7:33 f.; 16:5–9; 25:10; 33:10 f.) Jeremias speaks of "the voice of the bridegroom and the voice of the bride." When these "voices" or songs are heard, it is a sign of the Lord's favor, because conditions are such that people can marry and settle down; life goes on normally and fruitfully. But when they are not heard, it is a sign of his displeasure. People are not living a normal life; waste and desolation afflict the land. In only one of the passages does Jeremias declare that these songs shall be heard; it is to indicate that the people will be restored and life shall go on with its moments of joy and praise of God: "There shall be heard again the sound of mirth and the sound of gladness, the voice of the bridegroom and the voice of the bride . . ." (33:11). In the other passages the prophet threatens that the land will be devastated. Then the nuptial song is out of place; there is no longer peace or the joy of marriage: "I will remove from the cities of Juda and the streets of Jerusalem the sound of mirth and the sound of gladness, the voice of the bridegroom and the voice of the bride . . ." (7:34).

The question naturally arises: Have any of these songs been handed down to us in Hebrew literature? It would seem that the Canticle is the only example. For it is exactly "the voice of the bridegroom and the voice of the bride."

There is another, more obscure, reference to wedding songs in the writings of Osee. This great poet saw mirrored in the harlotry of his own wife the disobedience and infidelity which Israel showed to Yahweh (cc. 1–3). The prophet, speaking in the name of the Lord, describes how the Lord will win back Israel, his wayward spouse; he will find the way to her heart and bring about her restoration:

> So, I will allure her;
>   I will lead her into the desert
>   and speak to her heart. . . .
> She shall *respond* there as in the days of her youth,
>   when she came up from the land of Egypt (2:16 f.).

Yahweh recalls the days of Israel's youth, when she first gave herself to him — when, in the Sinai desert, she *responded*. It was then that she sang her love and pledged herself in the covenant with Yahweh, just as the betrothed Israelites did in their wedding songs, the lover alternating with the beloved. In this description of Israel as Yahweh's spouse who answers him, Osee seems to be referring to the wedding song, the voices of the bridegroom and the bride, that was so typical of Israelite marriage.

The understanding of the Canticle as a wedding song is also suggested by similar poems in ancient Egyptian literature. We know that Egyptian influence on Israel was considerable, even if evidence of direct borrowing is elusive. It has already been indicated that the greatest correspondence between the literature of the two nations is to be found in the wisdom literature. We find no strict parallelism between the Canticle and the "love" poetry of the Egyptians, such as has been pointed out above for the Teaching of Amen-em-Ope and Proverbs 22:17–24:22. But that is not necessary for determining the type of literature in the Canticle. We do find that both literatures agree in atmosphere, in similarity of metaphor and situations. For example, the voice of the swallow invites an Egyptian lass to the beauty of the countryside; in the Canticle, "the song of the dove is heard in our land" and it is a sign of spring (2:12 f.). An Egyptian youth finds that his love for his "sister" (compare Ct 4:9 f.; 4:12; 5:1 f. for this title for the beloved) works as a charm to bring him through dangerous waters infested by crocodiles; similarly in the Canticle, "Deep waters cannot quench love, nor floods sweep it away" (8:7). The themes of love-sickness (Ct 2:5; 5:8) and the absence of the loved one are common to the Israelite and Egyptian compositions. These comparisons, which could be duplicated in almost any "love" literature, confirm the opinion that the Canticle refers to the love of a man and woman. We are dealing with wedding songs that have been preserved with all the color and fervor which characterized the institution of marriage among the Israelites. The song is a mutual exchange of declarations of love and fidelity between two betrothed.

It might be thought that such a song would be out of place in a group of inspired books. This would be a shortsighted view. Our own Christian sacramental system proclaims the holiness of marriage. For the Israelites also marriage was a holy thing. They did not oppose, as we do, "profane" to "sacred"; nothing is profane because God touches all things. And as far as marriage is concerned, it was God himself who instituted it. It was the Lord who described the yearning of woman for man: "For your husband shall be your longing" (Gn 3:16). The Canticle is a living testimony to these words.

A Sapiential Book

Our song is grouped by Christian tradition among the Sapiential or Wisdom books, and this classification betrays no little insight into its message. The Israelite sages of the postexilic era are the persons most likely responsible for the preservation of this work. They were the great collectors of tradition relating to the Israelite way of life. According to custom, they attributed the book to Solomon, the patron of the wisdom literature. And in this way they also indicated their approval of the message that such a composition would carry to their fellow Israelites. A wholesome attitude to married love needed to be stated and restated in the postexilic period of Israel's history. General mistrust of women, even misogynism, is characteristic of writers of the Hellenistic era. Ecclesiastes makes the dour observation:

More bitter than death I find the woman who is a hunter's trap, whose heart is a snare and whose hands are prison bonds. He who is pleasing to God will escape her, but the sinner will be entrapped by her. Behold, this have I found, says Coheleth, adding one thing to another that I might discover the answer which my soul still seeks and has not found: One man out of a thousand have I come upon, but a woman among them all I have not discerned. Behold, only this have I found out: God made mankind straight, but men have had recourse to many subtleties (Eccl 7:26–29).

The woman he finds "more bitter than death" is not the sex, so much as it is a *type* well known in wisdom literature (Prv 5:1–14; 7:1–27, etc.). Only the virtuous will escape her, but the sinners will be caught by her. All this is quite in line with traditional advice. In justice to Coheleth it should be said that his observations bear on man in general. His mathematical ratio does not speak highly for the male, either; rather, his considered judgment is given upon the human race in the last line. He himself urged man to "enjoy life with the wife whom you love" (9:9).

Sirach, too, has some rather hard lines about women:

> Worst of all wounds is that of the heart,
>> worst of all evils is that of a woman . . .
> Wickedness changes a woman's looks,
>> and makes her sullen as a female bear.
> When her husband sits among his neighbors,
>> a bitter sign escapes him unawares . . .
> Depressed mind, saddened face,
>> broken heart — this from an evil wife.
> Feeble hands and quaking knees —
>> from a wife who brings no happiness to her husband.
> In woman was sin's beginning,
>> and because of her we all die (Sir 25:12–25).

However, if Sirach complained about a poor wife, he appreciated a good one; here is the reverse of the coin:

> A woman's beauty makes her husband's face light up,
>> for it surpasses all else that charms the eye;
> And if, besides, her speech is kindly,
>> his lot is beyond that of mortal men.
> A wife is her husband's richest treasure,
>> a helpmate, a steadying column.
> A vineyard with no hedge will be overrun;
>> a man with no wife becomes a homeless wanderer
>>> (36:22–25).

There is a notable similarity of language and ideas between a passage in the book of Proverbs and the Canticle:

> Drink water from your own cistern,
>   running water from your own well.
> How may your water sources be dispersed abroad,
>   streams of water in the streets?
> Let your fountain be yours alone,
>   not one shared with strangers;
> And have joy of the wife of your youth,
>   your lovely hind, your graceful doe.
> Her love will invigorate you always,
>   through her love you will flourish continually
>
> (Prv 5:15–19).

The "cistern" and "running water" is reminiscent of the "garden fountain, a well of water flowing fresh" in Ct 4:15. The "water sources" that are not to be "dispersed aboard" resemble the "fountain sealed" of Ct 4:12. The metaphors of the hind and the doe are cut from the same cloth as the metaphors in the Canticle, gazelles, stags, hinds (2:7, 9, 17).

In view of the fact that polygamy and divorce were allowed in Israel, the ideal of perfect, exclusive, love between man and woman is all the more striking, and the Canticle gives voice to this ideal. The book of Malachy, also a postexilic work, provides additional evidence of this positive attitude toward marriage. After condemning mixed marriages (2:10–12), the prophet turns to divorce. The reason for their prayers being unanswered, he tells the people, is infidelity to their wives:

> For the Lord is witness between you
>   and the wife of your youth;
> You have been false to her,
>   although she is your companion and your wife by
>   covenant. . . .
> Have care for your spirit,
>   and do not be false to the wife of your youth.
> For I hate divorce,
>   says the Lord God of Israel. . . . (2:14–16)

Two points are quite clear: the role of God as a witness, and the charge of being false to the wife with whom the husband has covenanted. A different and deeper understanding of marriage appears here, and we may understand the Canticle of Canticles as reflecting the same spirit.

A Dramatic Poem

From what has been said about the Canticle as a song, one can appreciate its dramatic character. The lover praises the beloved for her beauty and her faithfulness; she responds with declarations of her love, or some other variation on the theme of love. The song proceeds in this manner from one scene to another. Yet, it is not a drama, as some have thought. We have no conflict, no build-up, such as is essential to drama. In fact, there is no example of the dramatic form in ancient Semitic literature. The song remains true to its origins: It is the "voice of the bride" and the "voice of the bridegroom," a dialogue between lovers. For this reason many modern translations follow a practice that is as old as the fourth century Codex Sinaiticus, and indicate by marginal notations (B, G, D) that the lines are spoken by the Bride, the Groom, or the Daughters of Jerusalem.

This dialogue character of the Song brings with it certain difficulties in understanding the thread of thought. There are frequent and abrupt transitions from one situation to another. This very fact, coupled with our explanation of the origins of the composition, suggests that we have more than one song here. When the Canticle was finally written down and reduced to some unity by the Israelite sages, it incorporated snatches of dialogue that had originally been uttered by various persons in varying situations. This would account for the frequent lack of unity which we shall see within the canticle itself. Yet, the wisdom teacher who put the Canticle in its final, inspired form succeeded in stamping it with a certain unity by means of the repetition of verses (e.g., 2:6–9 and 8:3 f.) and by the repetition of situations (3:1–5 and 5:2–8).

The Canticle is more an expression of a mood than a carefully constructed theme. There is really no climax in it and none is needed. The marriage relationship itself is the climax; the whole purpose is to express this, to capture it as it existed among the people. So there is no plot, no conflict, but a series of scenes taken from real life. There can be no question, therefore, of a development in the mutual love of the lover and the beloved; the two are as much in love at the beginning of the Canticle as at the end. Even the beautiful lines of 8:6 f. are not a climax; these sentiments simply reflect the Israelite attitude toward marriage and love, and come quite naturally within the scope of the poem.

A Song in Imagery

The Hebrews thought in terms of the concrete, and the Canticle is an example of vivid, real-life imagery which came so readily from the lips of these people. Geography for them is a living thing: Cedar, Salma, Engaddi, Saron, Lebanon, Hermon, Galaad, Thirsa, Hesebon. The mention of these towns and mountains show the Hebrew feeling for the Palestinian countryside. The choice of vocabulary suggests an atmosphere that is close to the life and loves of the common man: vineyards and wine, perfume and spice beds, gazelles and hinds, lilies and pomegranates, doves and foxes. Within this small poem (e.g., 2:10–14; 4:12–16; 6:11 f.; 7:12–14) is contained a great range of proper names which evoke pictures of all sorts. But you do not ask yourself if the Palestinian garden contained all the varied type of growth that is mentioned, for example, in 4:14:

> Nard and saffron, calamus and cinnamon,
>   with all kinds of incense;
> Myrrh and aloes,
>   with all the finest spices.

Neither can you apply pure reason to the descriptions of the physical charms; lips are not "red blossoms" dripping "choice myrrh." Yet, word-sounds, images, and personal experience combine to speak the unmistakable language of love.

As an aid to the understanding of this poem, we propose to give a brief summary of the course of the dialogue. The object is not to give a full interpretation, but simply to enable the reader to understand who is speaking and, in general, what he is saying.

The Course of the Dialogue

Love's Desires (1:2–4) strikes a note that runs throughout the entire poem: a desire for union with the Groom. At the very beginning there is evidenced a certain tension between the Bride and the Daughters. There is really no equality between them; the Bride alone is the beloved. But the Daughters serve as a foil in the unfolding of the themes of love. They, too, recognize the charm of the Groom and seek his company (1:4; cf. 6:1). The Bride pays him a compliment, typical of the highly figurative language in the Canticle, by comparing him to wine and perfume:

More delightful is your love than wine!

Your name spoken is a spreading perfume (1:2 f.).

In this poem the Groom's love is foremost; every other value, symbolized by the wine, is secondary.

Love's Boast (1:5 f.) is a defense of the girl's beauty; she is beautiful despite a swarthiness which she attributes to exposure to the sun as she worked in the vineyards. There is a clever play on "vineyard," which is a key word in the rest of the Canticle. If her brothers aimed to seclude her (8:8 f.) by assigning her to work, she nevertheless has lost her heart to her lover because she cared not for her own vineyard, herself.

Love's Inquiry (1:7 f.) marks a definite motif or theme in the poem: the search. This is an artful means of emphasizing her desire to be with her lover; instead of a repetition of flat statements that would soon lose their flavor, the author has cleverly worked in situations that highlight the search motif, as here and also in 3:1–5 and 5:2–8. It also allows the introduction of a new metaphor for the Groom. In verse 4 he was termed a king (an echo to this is found in the "Solomon" passage, 3:6–11); now he is a shepherd. It is well known that the modern Syrian wedding ceremonies portray the married couple as king and queen. But the metaphor of king yields to that of shepherd throughout most of the poem, in which the lover lives close to nature.

Love's Vision (1:9–11) is a momentary glance at the beloved, which describes her ornament rather than her person. She is decked out in spangles such as one would see on royal Egyptian chariotry.

Love's Union (1:12–2:7) begins with the Bride's description of her lover as a precious perfume and spices, which cling to her. In their rural trysting place the lovers exchange compliments and she delicately describes her feeling for him. He is incomparable among men and his gentle embrace makes her swoon. The adjuration to the Daughters of Jerusalem of 2:7, many times repeated (3:5; 8:4), seems to say that love is no artificial thing. As indicated above, there is a certain tension between the Bride and the Daughters; she gives them to understand that they cannot hope to awaken in her lover any interest. His love belongs entirely to her and cannot be diverted.

A Tryst in the Spring (2:8–17) is perhaps the most beautiful section in our poem on account of its vivid imagery and depth of feeling. The beloved pictures her lover speeding over the mountains to visit her, describes his impatient fumbling at the lattice to see if she is at home. Then the superb invitation to her to come forth, because spring with the awakening of the world of nature has arrived:

> Arise, my beloved, my beautiful one,
>   and come!
> For see, the winter is past,
>   the rains are over and gone.
> The flowers appear on the earth,
>   the time of pruning the vines has come,
>   and the song of the dove is heard in our land.
> The fig tree puts forth its figs,
>   and the vines, in bloom, give forth fragrance.
> Arise, my beloved, my beautiful one,
>   and come! (2:10–13.)

As he catches a glimpse of her in her mountain home, he compares her to a dove whose song reveals its presence on a hilly fastness; let her sing, too. She replies with an enigmatic couplet about the foxes that damage the blossoming vineyards. Her reply defies certain analysis; it may have been part of a popular proverb or song. But the symbol of vineyards usually refers to herself. Even while the line offers no evident meaning of itself, it stands as a reply to "let me hear your voice," and echoes the symbol of the vineyard to which we have already been introduced (1:6). One recognizes the fragile texture of these love situations within the poem. We are constantly presented with snatches of conversation, constantly changing from one scene to another (banquet hall, shepherd's camps, cypresses, mountains) in the make-believe world of love that the poem is describing. I say "make-believe," not to rule out actual scenes that the poet may have experienced or witnessed, but to indicate that he has transformed them in his poetical treatment and has actually introduced a bewildering variety of them. This moving scene ends with her proud affirmation of their mutual devotion, and an invitation to him to spend the day with her, enjoying her company.

Loss and Discovery (3:1–5) is an instance of the search motif, intended to portray their mutual love. Absence makes lovers unhappy, but when there is added to this the inability to find one's beloved, the suffering is intense. The Bride relates how one night she was compelled to seek him — in vain. Hurried, futile questions! Perhaps the city watchmen have seen him? Finally she finds him, never to let him go till she brings him to her mother's home. The repetition of 2:7 in 3:5 is a refrain which is appropriate here in so far as it stresses to the Daughters once more that he belongs to her, although she seemed to have lost him.

Regal State of the Bridegroom (3:6–11). Again, there is an abrupt change of locale, and the shepherd is, once more, a king — King Solomon, no less. His approach is likened to a desert caravan: he comes with precious spices, accompanied by the imposing royal guard. His beautiful carriage catches the eye of the women, and the Daughters describe the imposing sight.

The Charms of the Beloved (4:1–11) is the first of the Groom's fairly lengthy descriptions of the beauty of the Bride. From commentators on all sides one receives cautions: that Oriental descriptions are apt, even if quite different from our taste. That is certainly true, but it should also be said that we are perhaps more literal minded about our metaphors. We literally see "a flock of goats streaming down the mountains of Galaad," and we remain without any reaction (although it is a scene that gladdens the heart of a shepherd and it has its own charm for anyone who has glimpsed such idyllic scenes in Palestine). Again, the Western mind may find it difficult to compare a neck to David's tower, decorated with a thousand shields; the nobility of carriage, if not the maiden's personal adornment, is the point of comparison. Such a description of the physical appearance of a girl is frequent in Semitic literature, and this literary type is still found in Palestinian folk songs today, where it is technically called a *waṣf*, from the Arabic word meaning "to describe." This description, as well as others within the song, is essentially chaste and reverent. The statements about the various parts of the body are not in bad taste in Semitic culture. The extreme erotic allusions and interpretations that have been construed by some modern scholars are the result of unhealthy critical judgment and a lack of insight on an artistic level. The description closes with a significant allusion to the invitation which the Bride has already issued to the Groom (cf. 4:6 with 2:17). Such allusions and interlockings indicate that the Canticle is meant to be a single poem, even though it incorporates several practices from the wedding *mores* of the day, and despite the fact that there are several switches from one scene to another without any transition.

The invitation (4:8–11) to the Bride to come from Lebanon is an outstanding example of sudden change. There is no logic to these switches in locale; in fact, they suggest that the author is incorporating some extraneous material into his work. At any rate, the effect is excellent; we are again in the mood of the mountains and hills of 2:8–17, when the lover issues his invitation:

Come from Lebanon, my bride,
   come from Lebanon, come!
Descend from the top of Amana,
   from the top of Sanir and Hermon,
From the haunts of lions,
   from the leopards' mountains.
You have ravished my heart, my sister, my bride;
   you have ravished my heart with one glance of your eyes,
   with one bead of your necklace.
How beautiful is your love, my sister, my bride,
   how much more delightful is your love than wine,
   and the fragrance of your ointments than all spices!
                           (4:8–10.)

The ardor of his love matches hers, and he returns the compli-
mentary comparison that she used of him in 1:2 — love more delightful than wine.

   The Lover and His Garden (4:12–5:1). The Groom's description of his Bride stresses first her inviolability and faithfulness: an
enclosed garden, a fountain sealed. Then he develops the metaphors of garden and (ever present in an oriental garden) fountain: choice fruits and spices, and fresh water such as one has
on the cool snowy heights of Lebanon. Here is a dear possession he
may well be proud of; may her charms captivate all. With a delicate
allusion to her gift of herself to him, she invites him into *his* garden
to partake of its offerings. His possession of her is affirmed in 5:1,
and also acclaimed by the Daughters of Jerusalem, "Drink freely
of love!"

   A Fruitless Search (5:2–8) is a companion piece to 3:1–5, using
the "search" motif. Again, there is the lover's visit and his call to
open; this time she fails to open quickly enough and he has already departed. The girl's reply to her lover's request is strange.
But in the context it is clear that her devotion to him has not
diminished; in the very next verse she is trembling joyfully in
anticipation of her lover. The "irrationality" of her reply in verse 3
must be attributed to her high emotion at the time. It is psycho-
logically plausible that a person under emotional stress can be be-

fuddled before a course of action which in a calm state would present no problem. The search begins when she discovers his departure, but this time she is beaten by the city watchmen (the significance of this detail is hard to appraise). Finally, she has recourse to the Daughters to find her lover. They are to inform him that she is faint with love. It should be emphasized that this is, once more, a love-situation, artfully contrived. The sole purpose for appealing to the Daughters is to create movement within the poem and to give the Daughters their cue to ask for a description of the lover, which is related in the next unit.

The Charms of the Lost Lover (5:9–16). The reason for the question asked by the Daughters is to give the Bride an opportunity to praise her lover's beauty. As we have already noted concerning such descriptions, the taste is oriental; the main parts of the body are mentioned and briefly described (in terms of the Jerusalem temple? e.g., ivory, marble, cedars).

Discovery (6:1–3). It now becomes apparent that the lover was not really lost. The whole episode is part of the make-believe of the artist's world. The question raised by the Daughters amounts to a claim they make for him. They, too, will assist in the search; where has he gone? The question may seem foolish after the Bride has just asked them. But the point of the question is not the actual location of the hero, but the interest in him which has been awakened in the hearts of the Daughters; they are ready to join in the search. The Bride's answer is a startling one; her lover is in "his garden" — herself:

> My lover has come down to his garden,
> 　to the beds of spice,
> To browse in the garden
> 　and to gather lilies.
> My beloved belongs to me and I to him:
> 　he browses among the lilies (6:2 f.).

In other words, he was never really lost; he was and remains hers. The whole situation of loss and discovery is a device leading up to the affirmations of the Groom's fidelity to his Bride.

The Charms of the Beloved (6:4–10) are related in a *waṣf* that uses many of the same metaphors in the previous description. The comparison to Thirsa (6:4), the early capital of the Northern Kingdom, is perhaps a play on the word, which is to be derived from the Hebrew term meaning "pleasing." As the Bride once pronounced him unique among men, he now returns the compliment: "One alone is my dove, my perfect one." And this is proved by the fact that all women sing her praises.

Love's Meeting (6:11 f.) is the gist of two verses that are the most difficult in the poem; verse 12 is textually uncertain, and the whole constitutes an unusually abrupt transition from the preceding context. It seems to describe another rural scene when a great transformation was effected in the Bride; it was because of something that occurred in relation to her lover (the first inkling that her affection was returned?) that she recognized herself as "the blessed one of my kinswomen."

The Beauty of the Bride (7:1–6) is introduced by a summons to dance, issued by the Daughters to the "Sulamite," i.e., the Bride. One is tempted to understand the term Sulamite as an artificial name, parallel to the name Solomon which is used of the Groom; but it may also be related to the town of Sunem in the plain of Esdrelon. The coy reply of the girl to the Daughters' invitation indicates that she does not want to make herself a spectacle. Thereupon the Daughters launch into a description of the Bride that is noticeably different from those previously uttered by the Groom. Whereas the other descriptions started from the head down, this one begins with the feet. Moreover, it emphasizes, in metaphors that are not precise to us, the fertility that is wished for the Bride (v. 3).

Love's Desires (7:7–10), uttered by the Groom, match the opening verses of the Canticle which were spoken by his beloved. The lover expresses his admiration and desire for union with her in the symbol of the vine cluster, and his final word is turned into a protestation of loyalty and devotion by the Bride, who completes his words (v. 10).

Love's Union (7:11–8:4) begins with an invitation by the Bride
to retire to the country and this recalls the vineyard theme:

> Let us go early to the vineyards, and see
>   if the vines are in bloom,
> If the buds have opened,
>   if the pomegranates have blossomed;
> There will I give you my love (7:13).

In 8:1 ff., she expresses a new desire: if only he were her brother,
they might manifest their mutual affection even in public, without
any fear of taunt. He could be a member of her own household,
enjoying her presence continually. The scene closes exactly like
the previous section of the same title (1:12–2:7).

Homecoming (8:5) is the title of a single verse in which the
Daughters hail the approach of the couple, while the Groom recalls the first trysting place: at home.

True Love (8:6 f.) has never been better described than in
these lines:

> Set me as a seal on your heart,
>   as a seal on your arm;
> For stern as death is love,
>   relentless as the nether world is devotion;
>   its flames are a blazing fire.
> Deep waters cannot quench love,
>   nor floods sweep it away.
> Were one to offer all he owns to purchase love,
>   he would be roundly mocked (8:6 f.).

The seal, worn as it was around the neck or on the finger, aptly
expresses her affection; its use for signatures and identification
shows that it is a symbol for the person. The comparison between
love and death emphasizes the relentless pursuit of each for its
proper object. Nothing staves off death; neither can love be de-
feated by the greatest obstacles.

Chastity and Its Welcome (8:8–10) begins with the Bride
quoting what her brothers have said about her. Once they had put
her to work in the vineyards (1:6) as a protective measure. They

are concerned about her youth and marriage prospects; she needs to be protected. They will test her: if she is of easy virtue (a door), they shall guard her doggedly; but if she is virtuous (a wall), they will reward her. Her proud answer to this is that she is a wall; she has been chaste and this has made her welcome to her lover.

The Bride and Her Dowry (8:11 f.) is widely regarded, along with the final verses of chapter eight, as an addition to the Canticle; it is certainly difficult to understand. The heading suggests that a dowry is in question here. The Groom, referred to once more as "Solomon," is said to possess a most valuable vineyard, valued at a thousand silver pieces. Then the Bride refers to her own vineyard which is at her own disposal. As we have noted before, the vineyard is a symbol for herself. Her own vineyard seems to be the same as Solomon's which was given over to the caretakers (her brothers). She now proclaims that this vineyard belongs to Solomon, with a thousand pieces for dowry that she is bringing him, and there is a settlement of two hundred pieces for her brothers.

Life Together (8:13 f.) is an unusual ending, yet it is somehow characteristic of the sudden movement throughout the Song. The Groom asks to hear her voice, as he did once before (2:14 f.), and she replies with a phrase that she has used before, when she invited him to stay with her (2:17).

The Interpretation

It is clear from what has already been said that this poem, taken in the literal sense as a nuptial song, is concerned with the mutual love of two human beings. For this reason it has a particular appeal for every married couple; the exchanges between lover and beloved exemplify the affection and fidelity which is proper to the married state. Loyalty and devotion encourages them to find only what is beautiful and admirable in each other.

However, we cannot take leave of the Canticle without noting another interpretation that has deep roots in both Jewish and Christian tradition. According to this point of view, there is a deeper meaning to the song; it describes the love of God for his

People — Yahweh and Israel, Christ and the Church. It is true that the poem makes no direct allusion to God and people. Nevertheless, it can be argued, the theme of human love is a two-edged sword in the Old Testament. It can be understood in and by itself, with reference to man and woman, as we have seen. But it is also applied to divine love, and this figure of the marriage between God and his people is one of the great themes in both the Old and the New Testament.

The prophet Osee is the first we know of to describe the covenant relationship between God and Israel as a marriage. In fact, his own tragic marriage may have suggested the application. He was married to an adulteress, Gomer, who begot three children. In this experience the prophet saw mirrored a greater betrayal, the betrayal of Yahweh by his unfaithful people; Gomer's harlotry is matched by Israel's infidelity. Hence the symbolic names which Osee gave to the children: *Yezreel* (God scatters); *Lo-Ruhama* (Not to be pitied); and *Lo-Ammi* (Not my people): the nation of Israel will be pitilessly scattered through the world, for they are unworthy to be God's people.

This theme is taken up by many later prophets, Isaias, Jeremias, and Ezechiel. The most bitter denunciations of the nation are couched in terms of marital infidelity. With biting irony, Isaias says of Jerusalem:

> How has she turned adulteress,
>   the faithful city, so upright!
> Justice used to lodge within her,
>   but now, murderers (1:21).

In Jeremias 3:1, God remonstrates with his people:

> And you, who have played the harlot with many lovers,
>   would you dare return to me?

Ezechiel tells the parable about Jerusalem in chapter 16, and about the two sisters (Israel and Juda) in chapter 23. Yahweh lavished tender care upon Jerusalem from her childhood until she came to the "age of love." Then she played the harlot, and for that she shall be turned over to her "lovers" who will devastate her land and leave her naked.

But the metaphor is not all darkness; the espousals will be renewed one day, and then, as Osee puts it,

> I will espouse you to me forever:
> I will espouse you in righteousness and in justice;
> in love and in mercy;
> I will espouse you in fidelity,
> and you shall know the Lord (2:21 f.).

In a bold verse of Isaias, the relationship between Yahweh and the new, purified, Israel is described:

> No more shall men call you "Forsaken,"
> or your land "Desolate,"
> You shall be called "My Delight,"
> and your land "Espousals."
> For the Lord delights in you,
> and makes your land his spouse.
> For as a young man marries a virgin,
> your Builder shall marry you.
> And as a bridegroom rejoices in his bride
> so shall your God rejoice in you (62:4 f.).

God is a bridegroom enjoying the happiness that a husband finds in a faithful wife. Note how the prophet stresses the attitude of Yahweh to his spouse. He *rejoices* in her. That is precisely the mood of the Canticle.

In view of this great literary tradition, it is not surprising that the theme is continued and developed in the New Testament. Speaking of Christ's love for the Church, St. Paul says that Jesus loved the Church and delivered himself up for her "in order to bring the church to himself in all her beauty, without a flaw or a wrinkle or anything of the kind, but to be consecrated and faultless. That is the way husbands ought to love their wives . . ." (Eph 5:27 f.). In his visions, St. John was told he would be shown "the bride, the wife of the Lamb" (Ap 21:9).

Not only the New Testament writers, but many later Christians, as St. Bernard and St. John of the Cross, have developed this deeper meaning of the Canticle. It is only what we might expect, because the love that exists in the human heart is a faint reflection of the God who, as St. John tells us (1 Jn 4:16), is *Love*.

6. THE "THOUGHTS" OF COHELETH

"WHAT does it profit a man, if he gain the whole world, but suffer the loss of his own soul?" This pointed question of Christ (Mt 16:26) was almost anticipated by Ecclesiastes, or Coheleth, some three hundred years before him. Yet there is a tremendous difference between this question of Christ and the many directed at this life by Coheleth; he would not have understood the meaning of "losing one's soul"; he did not know of a blessed immortality in the next life. But he did know the hard facts of life and found them not to his liking: "All is vanity and a chase after wind." The comparison to Christ's words is justified, however, by the bold and piercing evaluation passed on the things of this world by Coheleth. He is negative, or better iconoclastic, but he may well be read with a Christian accent.

This original thinker belonged to the class of wisdom teachers in Israel whose rich gnomic lessons have been preserved in books like Proverbs and Sirach. Yet he stands in sharp contrast to these writers by his insistence upon experience, upon observation. Whereas the sages were largely appraisers and collectors of the wisdom of the East, Coheleth was bent on assaying traditional values by the experimental method. This is evident in every chapter of his little work; only rarely does he stop to deliver a *bon mot* in the style of the traditional Hebrew sage. He is essentially an observer and tester of what takes place on the stage of life:

> I, Coheleth, was king over Israel in Jerusalem, and I applied my mind to search and investigate in wisdom all things that are done under the sun (1:12 f.).

Coheleth lived after the exile, at the time that Persian domination of the Near East passed into the hands of Alexander the Great and his successors. The strange name by which he is known is perhaps appropriate; it is as mysterious as his own identity. While it is derived from *cahal*, meaning "assembly," or "congregation," the precise meaning of *cohelet* is unknown; "leader of the assembly" and "preacher" are among the meanings suggested. All we know of him is contained in two verses (12:9 f.) of the epilogue to his book. One of his students, most likely, tells us that he was a sage, teaching and scrutinizing the traditional wisdom in his search for truth. He himself used a pseudonym: Son of David, King in Jerusalem. In this he followed the tradition of much of ancient Jewish literature, selecting a famous personage as his *nom de plume*. Who more than Solomon (3 Kgs 3:12) was renowned for wisdom? To lend dignity and power to his message, he chose to speak with the authority of this king. The disguise is only thinly veiled and not intended to deceive anyone; there are hints that he was not that historical character, as when he refers boastfully to having acquired more wisdom than all who were before him in Jerusalem; David was the only Israelite king who preceded him.

The reader must reconcile himself to great freedom and looseness employed in the writing of this book. It is not a dramatic dialogue, as Job, with a certain development and consistency. It belongs rather to the genre of Pascal's *Pensées,* or Thoughts: reflections and jottings of a mature man on the meaning of life, edited and perhaps to a certain extent reworked by one of his students. Coheleth may develop a theme logically for several verses, e.g., the vanity of wisdom (1:12–18) or of wealth (5:9–16), but he will also communicate his ideas in a series of pithy and obscure proverbs (9:18 ff.). Nor is he above giving out apparent contradictions: from one point of view, happier are the dead who have gone on, than those who still live (4:2); but then, "a live dog is better off than a dead lion" (9:4). These discrepancies are all the more disconcerting when they are juxtaposed. Thus, he points out (4:5 f.) that the fool folds his arms in laziness and in the same breath he adds that one handful, if one has tranquillity and ease, is better than both hands full, with toil! No one more than he was aware of the limited truth that proverbs possess. It is characteristic of him to balance them off against each other. We do the same thing ourselves when we say, "absence makes the heart grow fonder," but we also recognize that "out of sight, out of mind." He deliberately contrasts proverbs by way of pointing up the ultimate bankruptcy of wisdom — the vanity of it all.

This is typical of the constantly shifting point of view that makes him so fascinating and challenging. It is also one reason why he has been charged with skepticism, pessimism, hedonism, and any number of variant philosophies. Radicals as well as conservatives claim him. The famous German poet, Heinrich Heine, described the book as the "quintessence of skepticism," but Franz Delitzsch, a biblical scholar and compatriot of Heine, called it the "quintessence of piety." The truth lies somewhere in between. Coheleth would be the first to admit that he has not succeeded in presenting a finished philosophy of life. He is groping through the conflicting facts of experience and belief. At one moment he pursues a theme in a pessimistic mood, analyzing it for every possible disadvantage; then he will shrug it off with a perfunctory recommendation to enjoy the good things as they come (e.g., 8:15). He is unsteady, unsure of himself, continually thinking around and through his problem, adding one paradox to another, straining for a satisfactory conclusion.

The discrepancies discovered in Coheleth have led several scholars to detect various hands in the actual composition. The great part would be his, but a sage or Coheleth's disciples would have added to it several poetic verses. A Ḥasid, or pious man, would have been responsible for making certain additions to counterbalance some bold statements of the master that might shock his readers. Another writer would have added the epilogue (12:9–14) which speaks of Coheleth in the third person. This procedure takes care of the inconsistencies in the book, eliminating every discordant note. But is it really necessary? Rather than have recourse to such precarious conjecture, it seems better to explain the book all of one piece. Man is not a logical treatise and life is very complicated. So, at least, Coheleth thought; and he communicated this in a series of observations which he himself must have recognized as incomplete, although he could not deny them. In other words, much of his book is tentative; he is looking for a solution without stressing the absolute validity of many of the observations which he puts forth.

No one will ever succeed in giving a satisfactory outline of the contents of this book. Any scheme superimposes upon the meditations of Coheleth a framework that he certainly never had in mind. Once we recognize that these are jottings, unified only by the very tenuous thread of "vanity," an outline ceases to reflect the real thought and mood of the book. All will allow that there is a thesis, one dominant idea, in our book: everything in this life is vanity and pursuit of wind (e.g., 1:2 f.; 1:14; 2:11; 2:26, etc.). Hence one must take things as they come and enjoy the small pleasures that God allows (2:24; 8:15, etc.). Coheleth writes up and down this theme.

Man and Regularity (1:1–9; 3:1–11)

Regularity in nature and human life had a gloomy fascination for Coheleth. He drew bitter conclusions from the ceaseless round of events in nature. There is a perpetual and monotonous cycle of beginning all over again, which epitomizes man's own activity: the rising and setting of the sun, the back-and-forth movement of the wind, the continual flow of rivers to the sea (1:5–7). Can there be anything more sterile than the relentless push of nature? It is always the same, and so is man's achievement: "What has been, will be; what has been done, that will be done. Nothing is new under the sun" (1:9). It is not for us moderns to carp at the examples he chooses. He is not quarreling with the activity in nature as such; rather, this activity simply mirrors the monotony and sameness in human life, which is the real burden of his complaint:

> The eye is not satisfied with seeing,
> nor is the ear filled with hearing (1:8).

The regular flow of events can be considered from another point of view, that of time:

There is an appointed time for everything,
   and a time for every affair under the heavens.
A time to be born, and a time to die;
   a time to plant, and a time to uproot the plant. . . .
A time to love, and a time to hate;
   a time of war, and a time of peace (3:1–8).

The catalogue of activities, which have their appointed *time*, stands
in contrast to man in whose heart God has put *timelessness*.
Precisely because man has this sense of the timeless, he fails to
make sense of the timely. He is unable to discover, "from beginning
to end, the work which God has done" (3:11). Coheleth has
merely stated this contrast, without developing its meaning. If
we understand his thought correctly, he means to say that man's
restless searching goes beyond the regularity that he sees in the
world. In fact, from man's point of view, the regularity is only
apparent. The timelessness in his own heart does not square with
the individual units of time; he is out of kilter with the events
that are timed and governed by God and his Providence.

Vanity of Pleasure (2:1–12; 6:7–9) and Riches (5:9–6:6)

Coheleth describes at great length his pursuit of pleasure. This
was a careful experiment, guided by wisdom, for the purpose of
finding out "what is best for men to do under the heavens during
the limited days of their life" (2:3). In a setting reminiscent of the
splendors of Solomon's reign (e.g., 3 Kgs 4:22 f.; 9:21–23), he
details the riches he acquired, the buildings he constructed, the
lavish life that he adopted: "Nothing that my eyes desired did I
deny them, nor did I deprive myself of any joy . . ." (2:10). But
he could not bring it off. He was deep enough to see that no real
satisfaction lies in these pleasures, especially from the practical
viewpoint of man's insatiable appetite: ". . . all man's toil is for his
mouth, yet his desire is not fulfilled" (6:7).

When one considers the precarious grasp that man has on his
possessions, the vanity of riches is apparent. In his own experience
Coheleth had learned of various instances. A man died before he

could enjoy his riches, and a stranger was the heir. Even the fate of a stillborn infant is better than his! The infant, at least, has not been wounded by life, crushed in death by disappointment; a merciful darkness has shrouded it (6:1–6). There was also the man who lost in an evil mishap the treasure he amassed. He dies a failure, with nothing to leave to his heir, as naked and destitute as he entered into the world (5:12–16). But even when there is none to inherit, the situation is not improved: "For here is a man who has labored with wisdom and knowledge and skill, and to another, who has not labored over it, he must leave his property" (2:21). Thus Coheleth proceeds, ricocheting from one cushion to another, balancing off an alleged advantage against a clear disadvantage. It is not that Coheleth favored a lonely life without heirs. He found it a vanity that a solitary man, without son or brother, should toil only to find that his riches would not satisfy his greed (4:7 f.). "Woe to the solitary man! For if he should fall, he has no one to lift him up" (4:10). Thus a neat dilemma has been set up: work for riches, but leave them to another; yet, even were you to be alone with them, they would not satisfy you. In fact, Coheleth recognizes no real value in man's work: "All toil and skillful work is the rivalry of one man for another" (4:4).

Vanity of Wisdom (1:12–18; 2:13–17; 7:1–25; 8:16–17; 9:13–17; 12:9–14)

Is it possible for a man to believe in himself and in his vocation, and yet decry his calling? In a sense, that is what Coheleth does. He recognizes the achievement of his profession as a wisdom teacher, yet he is sharpsighted and honest enough to call the pursuit of wisdom "vanity." He was able to boast that he had acquired more wisdom than all who had been before him in Jerusalem, that his "mind had broad experience of wisdom and knowledge" (1:16). The student who edited his book has vividly described his master at work:

Besides being wise, Coheleth taught the people knowledge, and weighed, scrutinized and arranged many proverbs. Coheleth sought to find pleasing sayings, and to write down true sayings with precision. The sayings of the wise are like goads; like fixed pegs are the topics given by one collector (12:9–11).

But both teacher (1:18) and disciple (12:12) appreciated the difficulty of their vocation:

> In much wisdom there is much sorrow,
>   and he who stores up knowledge stores up grief (1:18).

True, he recognizes a certain theoretical superiority in the wise man. He has eyes in his head, whereas the fool walks in darkness (2:14); it is the advantage of light over darkness. He complained that others did not recognize this and recalled an episode where a poor man's wisdom saved a city from the mighty attack of a king — without recognition: "Though I had said, 'wisdom is better than force,' yet the wisdom of the poor man is despised and his words go unheeded" (9:17).

However, the real difficulty that was ever present to Coheleth was the fact that wisdom is inaccessible: "I said, 'I will acquire wisdom'; but is was beyond me. What exists is far-reaching; it is deep, very deep; who can find it out?" (7:23 f.) This is the theme we have seen developed so graphically in the twenty-eighth chapter of Job. You can find precious metals, even if they are in the bowels of the earth, but wisdom is nowhere to be found, in the abyss or in Abaddon. Only God knows the way to it, and man's only approach to it lies in "the fear of the Lord." But Coheleth's restless mind does not remain content with this convenient principle. It is not that he does not fear God (cf. 7:18; 8:12), but he has pushed the frontiers of wisdom beyond the plateau reached by earlier wisdom writers. It is in this advanced sphere that he acknowledges his failure to find out wisdom.

From a practical point of view, and one that was very personal to himself, he found that the pursuit of wisdom is vain because the same lot befalls the wise man and the fool; death is the enemy of wisdom:

I knew that one lot befalls both of them. So I said to myself, if the fool's lot is to befall me also, why then should I be wise? Where is the profit for me? And I concluded in my heart that this too is vanity. Neither of the wise man nor of the fool will there be an abiding remembrance, for in days to come both will have been forgotten. How is it that the wise man dies as well as the fool! (2:15 f.)

He could not resign himself to this deplorable equality, and his ideas on man's destiny deserve detailed treatment.

Man's End (3:19-21; 2:15 f.; 9:1-3; 12:7)

Coheleth goes so far as to admit an equality between man and beast:

For the lot of man and of beast is one lot; the one dies as well as the other. Both have the same life-breath, and man has no advantage over the beast; but all is vanity. Both go to the same place; both were made from the dust and to the dust they shall return. Who knows if the life-breath of the children of men goes upward and the life-breath of beasts goes earthward? (3:19-21.)

This famous passage has given rise to much misunderstanding. The first impression is that Coheleth has donned the robes of a modern materialist. It is precisely this transference of the Hebrew thinker into the modern philosophical sphere that is at fault. This is *not* speculative philosophy. Coheleth does not deny the realm of the spirit, as the materialist does. Neither does he deny the existence and differentiation of the human soul from the animal; he does not know the meaning of the philosophical term, soul.

This text is "difficult" only for one who equates life-breath with soul, as might be done by any modern reader who thinks along the lines of traditional Greek and Christian philosophy. But the Hebrew had no concept of "soul" as an independent spirit in man which is his animating principle. For him, man is not body and soul, he is animated body. The term life-breath (*ruᵃh* or *nᵉšamah*) is to be understood from Genesis 2:7; God "breathed into man's nostrils the breath of life" and man became a living being. This anthropomorphic description of the creative act betrays the Hebrew understanding of life. The sign of life was in the breath (compare the Latin *spiritus* from *spirare*); it was not merely that man, when he ceased to breathe, was dead; even when he slept or was unconscious, there was a mysterious breathing over which he had no control, and which came from elsewhere. This is described in Job 33:4:

> The *ruⁿh* (spirit) of God has made me,
> the *nᵉšamah* (life-breath) of the Almighty keeps me alive.

In the same book, Eliu points out how death ensues if God withdraws the life breath:

> If he were to take back his *ruⁿh* to himself,
> withdraw to himself his *nᵉšamah*,
> All flesh would perish together
> and man would return to the dust (Jb 34:14 f.).

Thus Coheleth is only voicing the traditional view. The life-breath of man and beast is taken away and they die. One cannot rightly infer from this that Coheleth teaches that both have the same nature. Such a philosophical question is foreign to him, nor is it posed as such in the entire Old Testament.

In 3:19–21 Coheleth perceives that there is no difference between man and beast as far as their final end is concerned. Lacking the later revelation concerning a blessed immortality, he can only affirm that man corrupts, and that is the end:

> The dust returns to the earth as it once was,
> and the life-breath returns to God who gave it (12:7).

Some thinkers of his day tried to draw a distinction between man and beast: the life-breath of man did not go downward like that of the beast, but upward. Who knows? Coheleth defiantly asks.

Coheleth's only mention of the nether world, or Sheol, is heartrending: "For there will be no work, nor reason, nor knowledge, nor wisdom in the nether world where you are going" (9:10). This description of a bleak existence tallies with other statements in the Old Testament regarding the afterlife. There are two points worth recalling here. First, no revelation concerning the afterlife was given to the Jews, although there are suggestions in the Psalms and finally a clear teaching in the book of Wisdom. Second, Israelite thinkers never posed the question of *how* man survives in Sheol, but they assert the fact that he does. Since man is an animated body, when he dies there seems to be nothing left that can cross the line of death. Nevertheless, the Hebrews placed the dead in Sheol. But since a dead man is obviously without the use of his body, it follows that this is hardly "life." It is "the land of darkness and of gloom, the black, disordered land, where darkness is the only light" (Jb 10:21 f.).

Some interpreters of the Old Testament claim that all this is tantamount to denying survival after death, that the gloomy statements about Sheol are only poetic descriptions of nonexistence. Even though the imaginative character of these descriptions is to be admitted, this view does not do justice to the belief in the nether world that is expressed in various parts of the Old Testament. For example, when David's son dies, the king says, "Now that he is dead, why should I fast? Can I bring him back again? I shall go to him, but he cannot come back to me" (2 Sm 12:23). Again, when the desperate Saul wishes to contact the dead prophet Samuel, he has recourse to the witch of Endor to bring the prophet back (1 Sm 28). The assumption is clear: Samuel exists in the nether world.

But no little care is needed in interpreting Old Testament passages that bear upon Sheol, since there is no consistent pattern worked out in the Bible. The fact is that the Hebrew did not have what we would consider a logical and clear concept of Sheol. It is given a spatial description and located in the depths of the earth (cf. Nm 16:23 f.), but it is also pictured as being a necropolis with graves (Ez 32:22–26). A living but sick psalmist can say that he is in Sheol (88:2–9; 69:2–4, 15 f.). Yet the Hebrew feels no contradiction in this concept. He can play fast and free with the location of the nether world because for him it is more of a state, the sphere of death, than a place. The grave and sickness are manifestations of Sheol; where they are Sheol is.

The incomplete character of divine revelation in the Old Testament is never more strikingly emphasized than in Coheleth's statements about the next world. The full revelation of man's nature and of blessed immortality was to be reserved for the book of Wisdom, and the lips of him who was Incarnate Wisdom, the Resurrection and the Life.

The Problem of Evil in This World
(3:14-16; 4:1 f.; 7:13-18; 8:5-13; 8:16-9:6)

On the whole, the Hebrew bowed humbly to the necessity of death and the fact of Sheol. Coheleth's complaint is not directed against this finality so much as it is against the problem of justice — ever the Hebrew problem — that is involved. The problem became particularly acute in the management of affairs in this world, and such bold thinkers as the author of the book of Job, the prophets Jeremias and Habacuc, rebelled. Why did evil triumph? Why did not God act on behalf of the upright?

Coheleth found no answer to these questions, but he did not shy away from them. His position is worthy of admiration: against all the facts, he *believes* that God will judge; but there is no denying the facts. . . .

The difficulty is that man's life comes to an end without God ever having intervened, in a discernible manner, to reward him, whether for good or for evil. Coheleth had knowledge of several cases of injustice:

> I saw wicked men approach and enter; and as they left the sacred place, they were praised in the city for what they had done. This also is vanity. Because the sentence against evildoers is not promptly executed, therefore the hearts of men are filled with the desire to commit evil — because the sinner does evil a hundred times and survives (8:10-12).

> And still under the sun in the judgment place I saw wickedness, and in the seat of justice, iniquity (3:16).

His complaint is that God does nothing to correct these wrongs:

Love from hatred man cannot tell; both appear equally vain, in that there is the same lot for all, the just and the wicked, for the good and the bad, for the clean and the unclean, for him who offers sacrifice and him who does not. As it is for the good man, so it is for the sinner. . . . Among all the things that happen under the sun, this is the worst, that things turn out the same for all (9:1-3).

Like Job, Coheleth could not accept the traditional Hebrew theory that God rewarded the good with prosperity and punished the evil with misfortune.

The astonishing thing is that he nevertheless affirms his faith in God — even in the very teeth of the cases which he instances: "and I said to myself, both the just and the wicked God will judge, since there is a time for every affair and on every work a judgment" (3:17; see 3:16, above). Again, "all this I have kept in mind and recognized: the just, the wise, and their deeds are in the hand of God" (9:1; see 9:1-3, above).

Some interpreters do not believe that this is the voice of Coheleth. Such pious reflections, they say, are due to another who felt obliged to soften the denial of justice in this world. This interpretation fails to do justice to Coheleth. He is not inconsistent with himself by affirming a belief in judgment; faith is not incompatible with facts. His judgment here is not an experimental judgment; it is an act of faith. He still believes that God will judge even while this remains a mystery to him, lying as it does outside his experience. (Even if one admits that a disciple of Coheleth wrote 12:9-14 with its strong affirmation of faith in God's justice and judgment, there is no reason to attribute all such statements in the book to the disciple. The disciple learned from the master.) Job's querulousness was not any the more lessened for his great act of faith in 19:25 ff. Neither is the sharpness of Coheleth's observations blunted by his clinging to belief in judgment while repudiating the traditional application of this doctrine to saints and sinners.

It is to be admitted that certain statements of Coheleth are difficult to reconcile with his bitter complaints, such as

... though indeed I know that it shall be well with those who fear God, for their reverence toward him; and that it shall not be well with the wicked man, and he shall not prolong his shadowy days, for his lack of reverence toward God (8:12 f.).

These verses at first sight suggest a rosier view of life than Coheleth elsewhere admits. But really, he says no more here than what he always considers an ultimate truth: fear God. God is above every law, and the only thing to do is to show him reverence (cf. 7:18; 12:13 f.). He says not a word about the manner in which "it shall be well with those who fear God" — for he does not know. But he believes that the wicked man will not escape God; his "lack of reverence" will not put him in any better position; his wickedness will not help him live any longer.

The entire passage of 8:5–13 is important for the understanding of Coheleth's attitude toward the traditional theory of retribution. He begins by quoting a traditional religious aphorism about virtue and judgment:

He who keeps the commandments experiences no evil, and the wise man's heart knows times and judgments (8:5 f.).

He agrees with this in its general tenor, "for there is a time and judgment for everything," as he has taken great pains to elaborate in 3:1 ff. But when? and how? This aphorism does not touch on practical day-to-day living: "the sinner does evil a hundred times and survives" (8:12). The facts of the world do not correspond to the doctrine of judgment which he acknowledges.

There is simply no telling how God is going to act:

For to whatever man God sees fit he gives wisdom and knowledge and joy; but to the sinner he gives the task of gathering possessions to be given to whatever man God sees fit (2:25 f.).

Being virtuous or sinful has nothing to do with these gifts. The exponents of the traditional theory were fond of saying that if the sinner did prosper he would eventually lose his riches to the just (Prv 13:22; 28:8). No, Coheleth, replies, but "to whatever man God sees fit."

The familiar conclusion about the fear of God appears again in 7:18 at the end of some rather obscure advice:

I have seen all manner of things in my vain days: a just man perishing in his justice, and a wicked one surviving in his wickedness. "Be not just to excess, and be not overwise, lest you be ruined. Be not wicked to excess and be not foolish. Why should you die before your time?" It is good to hold to this rule, and not to let that one go; but he who fears God will win through at all events (7:15–18).

Several commentators think that these words exemplify the golden mean, *ne quid nimis,* or *medio tutissimus ibis.* Don't be too good or too evil. But is this what Coheleth means? He begins with the facts: there is no connection between virtue or evil and a man's lot in life. Then he quotes two typical proverbs that are opposed as paradoxes (cf. the same practice in Prv 17:27–28; 26:4–5). The notion of being "just to excess" must mean striking a pose as a just man, making a parade of wisdom. Such a *poseur,* who claims to be wiser than he is, will be ruined, as is the teaching of many sayings in the book of Proverbs (Pride goes before disaster, etc.; cf. Prv 16:18; 18:12). "Wicked to excess" should not be construed to imply that some wickedness is acceptable (Coheleth recognizes that "there is no man on earth so just as to do good and never sin" 7:20). Excessive wickedness means an evil so great that God must exterminate the sinner (e.g., Her and Onan in Gn 38:7–10). In verse 18 Coheleth passes a judgment on these two proverbs. He is willing to recognize that disaster awaits the excesses that are mentioned, but he really does not know how this works out in reality. All he is sure of is that the godfearing will "win through at all events" (cf. 3:17; 8:12 f.; 12:13 f.).

Youth and Old Age (11:7–12:7)

One does not expect to find in a writer that is as pessimistic as Coheleth an encomium of youth. It is a tribute to his sense of balance that he could see youth in this light, even if it is appreciated only in contrast with old age. There is another descrip-

tion of old age that deserves to be noticed in this connection.
Barzillai, *il vecchio*, is accompanying David down to the Jordan
after Absalom's revolt has been quelled. The King invites him to
the royal palace in Jerusalem as a reward, and Barzillai replies,
"Do I have enough days to live, to go up to Jerusalem with the
king? I am eighty years old now. Can I tell the difference between
good and evil or taste what I eat or drink? Or can I still hear the
voices of male and female singers? Why should I be a burden to
my lord king?" (2 Sm 19:35 f.) Coheleth describes the dawning
realization of old age in a famous allegory:

> Remember your Creator in the days of your youth,
>   before the evil days come
> And the years approach of which you will say,
>   I have no pleasure in them;
> Before the sun is darkened,
>   and the light, and the moon, and the stars,
>   while the clouds return after the rain . . .
> Before the silver cord is snapped
>   and the golden bowl is broken,
> And the pitcher is shattered at the spring,
>   and the broken pulley falls into the well,
> And the dust returns to the earth as it once was,
>   and the life-breath returns to God who gave it (12:1–7).

In view of this, Coheleth gives the advice:

> Rejoice, O young man, while you are young
>   and let your heart be glad in the days of your youth.
> Follow the ways of your heart,
>   the vision of your eyes;
> Yet understand that as regards all this
>   God will bring you to judgment (11:9).

Conclusion (2:24 f.; 3:12 f.; 3:22; 5:17–19; 7:13 f.; 8:15; 9:7–10; 11:7–10)

Consider the work of God. Who can make straight what he
has made crooked? On a good day enjoy good things, and on an

evil day consider: Both the one and the other God has made, so
that man cannot find fault with him in anything (7:13 f.).

These words of Coheleth point the way to the series of practical
conclusions which run through his little work. He really surrenders;
he can find no answer to the questions he has been asking — all is
vanity. But man must live under this inexplicable rule of God.
What advice can be given him?

A practical rule of life echoes throughout his writing. It is almost
as if he were driven back to this conclusion after exhausting strug-
gles with the paradoxes of this life. No less than eight times he
sets down his conclusion. A typical statement runs as follows:

> Here is what I recognize as good: it is well for a man to eat and
> drink and enjoy all the fruits of his labor under the sun during
> the limited days of the life God gives him; for this is his lot.
> Any man to whom God gives riches and property, and grants
> power to partake of them, so that he receives his lot and finds
> joy in the fruits of his toil, has a gift from God. For he will
> hardly dwell on the shortness of his life, because God lets him
> busy himself with the joy of his heart (5:17–19).

There is no mistaking the resigned accent; this is the best one
can do with life. It is vanity, but it can be enjoyed. The little
pleasures in life are recognized as gifts of God which lead man
to gloss over the shortness and inadequacy of life. In view of the
emptiness of the nether world (9:10), man must make the best
of it while he really lives.

It is true that Coheleth's pronouncements are melancholic. But
we can understand this because of the limitations of his point of
view, and we have to admire the acuteness of his pessimistic
observations. Even when he urges that "it is better to go to the
house of mourning than to the house of feasting," he gives a good
reason for it: "That is the end of every man, and the living should
take it to heart" (7:2). Nevertheless, we must not lose sight of
the emphasis he places upon mirth and enjoyment. The statement
in 2:2, "Of laughter I said: 'mad!' and of mirth: 'what good does
this do?' " is not contradictory. It was in the course of his experi-

ment with luxury that he reached such a conclusion. But for life
in general, he advises:

> Therefore I commend mirth, because there is nothing good for
> man under the sun except eating and drinking and mirth; for
> this is the accompaniment of his toil during the limited days
> of the life which God gives him under the sun (8:15).

Coheleth's insistence on joy is a remarkable fact which suggests
that his pessimism may be something of a literary device, an
exaggeration directed to attract attention to the "divine dissatis-
faction," that it was his lot to experience in the affairs of this life.
It would be a mistake to rate him as merely pessimistic and
disappointed by life. Through his dour outlook and his groping in
the dark shine his honesty and sincerity in evaluating all things.
And his conclusions are still appealing, even in the full light of
Christianity.

7. SIRACH (ECCLESIASTICUS): A JERUSALEM SAGE

THE name of the author and the title and language of his book have enjoyed an odd fate. His name has been preserved in variant readings as "Simon, son of Jesus, son of Eleazar, son of Sira" (Hebrew) or "Jesus, son of Sirach" (Greek). The Latin term, *Ecclesiasticus,* refers to the book rather than the author, whatever be the origin of the term. Some scholars have thought this title was given to the book because of the use the early Church made of it for catechumens. But this is not certain; we are sure only that the first known appearance of the Latin title is in the writings of St. Cyprian (+ 258). Putting together the data from the Hebrew text and the Greek translation, scholars generally agree on the name of the author as Jesus ben Sira or Jesus Sirach.

As if the uncertainty surrounding his name were not enough, copies of his book simply dropped out of sight. It was saved from oblivion as far as the Church was concerned because of the Greek, Syriac, and Old Latin translations in which it was preserved. Historically, this strange fate is intelligible. The book was not accepted in the official Jewish canon of biblical writings and not much interest was shown in the original Hebrew text. But the Church did accept the book as inspired and preserved it. Apart from a few spurious medieval Hebrew copies, the Hebrew text was lost from sight from about the time of St. Jerome (*ca.* 400) until the thrilling discovery made by Solomon Schechter in 1896. At that time about two thirds of the Hebrew text was recovered in Cairo from a *geniza* of a medieval Jewish sect, the Karaites. The *geniza* served as a temporary storeroom of used and tattered biblical manuscripts, before they were properly disposed of; by sheer accident this storeroom had been walled over when renovations were made during the middle ages. Then a few fragmentary lines of the book were discovered among the fragments of the recently discovered Dead Sea Scrolls. However, the Hebrew text discovered in Cairo dates from the medieval period (about the eleventh century) and it is not always a pure text; it has many retroversions from the early Syriac, which itself was originally translated from the Hebrew.

We know well the origins of the Greek translation from the prologue which the translator wrote for the Greek version. Here we learn that the translator was Sirach's own grandson, who migrated to Egypt in the thirty-eighth year of Ptolemy VII Euergetes, that is, in 132 B.C. This enterprising young man undertook the translation, as he tells us, "for the benefit of those living abroad who wish to acquire wisdom and are disposed to live their lives according to the standards of the Law." Toward this end he spent "many sleepless hours of close application," but he begs his reader's indulgence for any failure on his part, "for words spoken originally in Hebrew are not as effective when they are translated into another language." He has left us a valuable description of his grandfather:

> Many important truths have been handed down to us through the Law, the Prophets, and the later authors; and for these the instruction and wisdom of Israel merit praise. Now, those who are familiar with these truths must not only understand them themselves but, as lovers of wisdom, be able, in speech and in writing, to help others less familiar. Such a one was my grandfather Jesus, who, having devoted himself for a long time to the diligent study of the Law, the Prophets, and the rest of the books of our ancestors, and having developed a thorough familiarity with them, was moved to write something himself in the nature of instruction and wisdom, in order that those who love wisdom might, by acquainting themselves with what he too had written, make even greater progress in living in conformity with the Divine Law.

Sirach's familiarity with the Old Testament Law, Prophets and Writings is evident in every chapter. His work is a striking example of the "anthological" style discussed above in connection with Proverbs 1–9. He was so deeply impregnated with the thoughts and expressions of the earlier biblical writings that they came naturally to him when he wished to express his own ideas. In a sense, the work was not written at any one time. Rather, it reflects a lifetime of meditating on and teaching the Old Testament. We are able to fix his dates in a broad manner. His praise of Simon the High Priest, "the greatest among his brethren, and the glory of his people" (50:1 ff.), seems to be the verdict of an eyewitness who has thrilled to the liturgical service of the temple. But he writes as though this glorious page in Israel's history is past. So we are beyond the year 200, the approximate time of the death of Simon II. It is easy to understand the author's enthusiasm for those days, for he is closing out his life in an ominous era. Hellenization has infected priests and people. Israel is subject to a foreign ruler and will shortly taste the cruel and despotic persecution of Antiochus Epiphanes IV (175–164). The Maccabean revolt (167) has not yet begun; Antiochus is probably already king, but the full weight of oppression has not been felt. Yet Sirach can proclaim:

> God indeed will not delay,
>   and like a warrior, will not be still
> Till he breaks the backs of the merciless
>   and wreaks vengeance upon the proud;
> Till he destroys the haughty root and branch,
>   and smashes the scepter of the wicked;
> Till he requites mankind according to its deeds,
>   and repays men according to their thoughts;
> Till he defends the cause of his people,
>   and gladdens them by his mercy (35:19–23).

Thus within the first few decades of the second century before Christ Sirach prepared and completed his book, and within the same century his grandson translated it into Greek.

Autobiographical References

The book of Sirach is of the type that can be begun at the end as well as at any other chapter. The contents are so diversified that there is no adequate division which is not somewhat artificial. Several scholars have proposed a division based on the poems in praise of wisdom or God which occur throughout the book (1:1; 4:11; 6:18; 14:20; 16:22; 24:1; 32:14; 39:12; 42:15). But this work is essentially a compendium, a *Summa* of the wisdom teaching of the Old Testament without any order. Sirach left for the final chapter a little acrostic poem which reveals much about himself. His pursuit of wisdom began at an early age; it was a prayerful, steadfast pursuit, one that could succeed only if his conduct was in line with wisdom itself:

> I fixed on her my soul's desires,
>   and with its cleansing, I discovered her (51:20).

But once he had tasted of wisdom, he knew he was lost to her. Then, imitating the familiar cry of wisdom in the Old Testament, he invites his readers:

> Come to me, you who need instruction,
>   and take your place in my school;
> How long will you be deprived of what you need,
>   how long will your souls remain quite parched? . . .
> Submit yourselves to her yoke,
>   let your souls bear her weight;
> For she is close to those who seek her,
>   and he who is earnest finds her.
> See for yourselves! I labored but a little for her sake,
>   and found great rest.
> Listen, children, to my teaching!
>   you will win silver and gold through me (51:23–28).

It was at a *beth hammidrash*, as he calls his school in 51:23, that he would have received his instruction about wisdom. In such a school he would have been taught by the *Sopherim*, or scribes, whose ranks he eventually entered. The *Sopher* was a diligent student of the Torah, the Prophets, and the Writings which make up the complex of the Old Testament and we have already seen Sirach described thus by his grandson. There was no one prouder of the class to which he belonged, as is clear from the lengthy comparison he makes between the scribe and the craftsmen (38:24–39:11). The various artisans — plowman, designer, smith and potter — are all necessary; "without them no city would be lived in." But the practical must yield to the eternal:

> How different the man who devotes himself
>   to the study of the Law of the Most High!
> He explores the wisdom of the men of old
>   and occupies himself with the prophecies (39:1).

But the scribe is no "armchair" philosopher. As Sirach points out:

> He is in attendance upon the great,
>   and has entrance to the ruler.
> He travels among peoples of foreign lands
>   to learn what is good and evil among men (39:4 f.).

And he states that he learned more than he could ever say from his own travels (34:11). Sirach's judgment on the life of an artisan shows that he was no intellectual snob. His judgment on the other patterns of life is forthright and reverent, but also an honest appraisal: These did not match the excellence of the scribe. Such a judgment well reflects his basic attitude toward human personality and talent:

> My son, with humility have self-esteem;
>   prize yourself as you deserve (10:27).

In another revealing passage Sirach calls himself a rivulet. The Law itself is a river, comparable to the great rivers of antiquity, overflowing with wisdom. Sirach liked to see himself as the channel through which this wisdom would flow and reach out to others:

> Now I, like a rivulet from her stream,
>   channeling the waters into a garden,
> Said to myself, "I will water my plants,
>   my flower bed I will drench";

And suddenly this rivulet of mine became a river,
    then this stream of mine, a sea.
Thus do I send my teachings forth shining like the dawn,
    to become known afar off.
Thus do I pour out instruction like prophecy
    and bestow it on generations to come
                  (24:28–31; cf. 33:16–18).

In contrast to the book of Proverbs with its verse units of thought, the wisdom of Sirach presents at times a whole chapter or more, dealing with one theme. We shall consider several themes that reflect certain value-judgments of Sirach and thus reveal more of the personality of this man: friends and friendship, speech, riches and poverty, Providence, women and marriage, the Law, and finally, the "praise of the Fathers."

Friends and Friendship

An outstanding characteristic of Sirach is his cautiousness. This is particularly evident in his judgments on friendship. Friends are to be *tested* (6:7). Too often, apparently, he had met the fair-weather type, who is a "friend when it suits him" but is not "true in time of distress."

Another is a friend, a boon companion,
    who will not be with you when sorrow comes.
When things go well, he is your other self,
    and lords it over your servants;
But if you are brought low, he turns against you
    and avoids meeting you (6:10–12).

It would seem that a bitter experience lies behind the cry that Sirach utters:

Is it not a sorrow unto death
    when your bosom companion becomes your enemy?
"Alas, my companion! Why were you created
    to blanket the earth with deceit?" (37:2–3.)

It is part of his cautiousness to measure friends by the yardstick of time; the true friend is an *old*, not a new one. A new friend is

like new wine: there is a taste only when it has aged (9:10). For
Sirach there is only one unforgivable sin in the matter of friendship — breaking confidence:

> Cherish your friend, keep faith with him;
>> but if you betray his confidence, follow him not;
> For as an enemy might kill a man,
>> you have killed your neighbor's friendship . . .
> A wound can be bound up, and an insult forgiven,
>> but he who betrays secrets does hopeless damage
>>
>> (27:17 f., 21).

It is entirely in the character of our author that he urges association
with the wise, the people of his own class:

> As best you can, take your neighbors' measure,
>> and associate with the wise.
> With the learned be intimate;
>> let all your conversation be about the Law of the Lord.
> Have just men for your table companions;
>> in the fear of God be your glory (9:14–16).

But he indicates that one's circle of friends should go beyond class
and be based on virtue; one is to associate with a religious man,
one who observes the commandments (37:12). As it works out,
this is practically a law of nature; as we would say, birds of a
feather flock together:

> Every living thing loves its own kind,
>> every man a man like himself.
> Every being is drawn to its own kind;
>> with his own kind every man associates.
> Is a wolf ever allied with a lamb?
>> So it is with the sinner and the just (13:14–16).

Sirach's attitude to friendship with the rich is typically careful.
He was too much a man of the world to be taken by mere prestige
or money. The rich man enslaves anyone he can use, only to
abandon him in the end:

> As long as you have anything he will speak fair words to you,
> and with smiles he will win your confidence;
> When he needs something from you he will cajole you,
> then without regret he will impoverish you.
> While it serves his purpose he will beguile you,
> then twice or three times he will terrify you;
> When later he sees you he will pass you by,
> and shake his head over you (13:5–7).

His experience with these men shows how keen and observant he was:

> When invited by a man of influence, keep your distance;
> then he will urge you all the more.
> Be not bold with him lest you be rebuffed,
> but keep not too far away lest you be forgotten.
> Engage not freely in discussion with him,
> trust not his many words;
> For by prolonged talk he will test you,
> and though smiling he will probe you.
> Mercilessly he will make of you a laughingstock,
> and will not refrain from injury or chains
>
> (13:9–12; cf. 8:1; 9:13).

On the other hand, his advice to make friends with the poor sounds badly motivated:

> Make fast friends with a man while he is poor;
> thus will you enjoy his prosperity with him (22:23).

But is this not less selfish than it appears? What selfish man would counsel friendship with the poor? The risk involved would make this attractive only to the unselfish. Hence personal enrichment is not so much a motive as a likely result; prove yourself a friend and reward will follow. This is because the Lord will reward the poor and the just:

> If you do good, know for whom you are doing it,
> and your kindness will have its effect.
> Do good to the just man and reward will be yours.
> if not from him, from the Lord (12:1–2).

Those whom Sirach would exclude from companionship, or even from any act of kindness, are sinners:

> No good comes to him who gives comfort to the wicked,
> nor is it an act of mercy that he does.
> Give to the good man, refuse the sinner;
> refresh the downtrodden, give nothing to the proud man.
> No arms for combat should you give him,
> lest he use them against yourself;
> With twofold evil you will meet
> for every good deed you do for him.
> The Most High himself hates sinners,
> and upon the wicked he takes vengeance (12:3–7).

This unyielding hatred of sinners is given a theological basis: The Lord hates sinners (12:7; 27:24). When one thinks of it, there is not much to be gained from the facile distinction between hating sin and loving the sinner. Sin does not exist in the abstract, but in the sinner; and the sinner, as such, is hateful. Moreover, in the Old Testament view of things, the sinner deserved punishment (in this life, the only life), so that God's justice might be preserved. Hence it was natural or even virtuous to wish to see this justice demonstrated. Who can say to what extent personal vengeance may have entered into this? But the essential fact should be recognized: The sinner is hated precisely as an enemy of God. As such he is deserving of hatred in the Christian dispensation as well, although this fact does not exclude Christ's recommendation to love enemies. The Old Testament did not reach this high level because it had gone as far as it could in trying to understand the mystery of suffering and injustice. Only the Crucified could utter the message of Matthew 5:43 ff.

Speech

Of no other human faculty does Sirach say as much as he does of the faculty of speech. Like the colorful language of St. James (3:4–10) is his appreciation of the power of that small but important organ of speech:

If you blow upon a spark, it quickens into flame,
  if you spit on it, it dies out;
  yet both you do with your mouth! (28:12.)

A blow from a whip raises a welt,
  but a blow from the tongue smashes bones;
Many have fallen by the edge of the sword,
  but not as many as by the tongue (28:17 f.).

Most of the time Sirach has in mind the typical catalogue of sins which are contrary to the eighth commandment of the Decalogue. Lying and inconstancy in speech are hateful to him (5:11–6:1; 20:24 f.). He was aware of the very human urge to disclose secrets and to indulge in gossip:

Let anything you hear die within you;
  be assured it will not make you burst.
When a fool hears something, he is in labor,
  like a woman giving birth to a child.
Like an arrow lodged in a man's thigh
  is gossip in the breast of a fool (19:9–11).

But knowledge of another's fault does oblige one to make fraternal correction where possible (19:12–16). Continual swearing by the Holy Name is also scored, as well as coarse and abusive language (23:7–13). Sirach displays a high sensitivity to foul language:

Their [i.e., sinners] oath-filled talk makes the hair stand on
    end,
  their brawls make one stop one's ears.
Wrangling among the haughty ends in bloodshed,
  their cursing is painful to hear (27:14 f.).

Basic to his ideas on the use of the tongue is the old and time-tested principle that conversation is the test of a man:

Praise no man before he speaks,
  for it is then that men are tested (27:7).

Providence

Sirach's view of life is clearly expressed in the following lines:

So from the first I took my stand,
    and wrote down as my theme:
The works of God are all of them good;
    every need when it comes he fills.
No cause then to say: "This is not as good as that";
    for each shows its worth at the proper time.
So now with full joy of heart proclaim
    and bless the name of the Holy One (39:32–35).

So, too, all men are of clay,
    for from earth man was formed;
Yet with his great knowledge the Lord makes men unlike;
    in different paths he has them walk.
Some he blesses and makes great,
    some he sanctifies and draws to himself.
Others he curses and brings low,
    and expels them from their place.
Like clay in the hands of a potter,
    to be molded according to his pleasure,
So are men in the hands of their Creator,
    to be assigned by him their function.
As evil contrasts with good, and death with life,
    so are sinners in contrast with the just;
See now all the works of the Most High;
    they come in pairs, the one the opposite of the other
                        (33:10–15).

God is supreme and has everything under control. This does not mean that man is not a free, responsible agent (cf. 15:11–20). In typical Hebrew fashion, both truths are upheld, but there is no attempt to explain how they fit together. The tendency is always to magnify the primary causality of God. Sirach finds a law of opposites inherent in reality: All the works of the Most High "come in pairs, the one the opposite of the other." This same law was also recognized by Coheleth (Eccl 7:14), but he was unable to balance them. The primary opposition is between good and evil, death and life (33:14), and here Sirach's basic optimism shines through. Instead of yielding to the pressure that evil and injustice exerted on men like Job and Coheleth, he finds a certain theoretical harmony in the world. Of course, evil is for sinners:

> Good things for the good he provided from the beginning,
>> but for the wicked good things and bad (39:25).

When evil afflicts the pious, this is a "testing":

> My son, when you come to serve the Lord,
>> prepare yourself for trials.
> Be sincere of heart and steadfast,
>> undisturbed in time of adversity.
> Cling to him, forsake him not;
>> thus will your future be great.
> Accept whatever befalls you,
>> in crushing misfortune be patient;
> For in fire gold is tested,
>> and worthy men in the crucible of humiliation.
> Trust God and he will help you;
>> make straight your ways and hope in him (2:1–6).

This passage shows that Sirach did not close his eyes to the hard facts. The only way he can rise above these obstacles is affirming his faith, as in 2:4–6. Like Job he submits, but without any satisfying encounter with God.

Sirach's thoughts on death are expressed most poignantly and beautifully (41:1–4). The thought of death can be only bitter for a man who has made a success of life, but how welcome the sentence for the weak, the cynical, and the despairing!

> Fear not death's decree;
>> remember it embraces those before you, and those after.
> Thus God has appointed for all flesh;
>> why then should you reject the will of the Most High?
> Whether one has lived a thousand years, a hundred, or ten,
>> in the nether world he has no claim on life (41:3 f.).

But Sirach will not tolerate undue grief on the occasion of some-one's death:

> Weeping bitterly, mourning fully,
>> pay your tribute of sorrow, as he deserves,
> One or two days, to prevent gossip;
>> then compose yourself after your grief (38:17 f.).

This extremely practical attitude is justified by the clear reasoning of a wisdom teacher:

> For grief can bring on an extremity
>> and heartache destroy one's health.
> Turn not your thoughts to him again;
>> cease to recall him; think rather of the end.
> Recall him not, for there is no hope of his return;
>> it will not help him, but will do you harm.
> Remember that his fate will also be yours;
>> for him it was yesterday, for you today.
> With the departed dead, let memory fade;
>> rally your courage, once the soul has left (38:19–23).

Man's lot in life is dour; he is plagued by all kinds of miseries and heartaches:

> A great anxiety has God allotted,
>> and a heavy yoke, to the sons of men;
> From the day one leaves his mother's womb
>> to the day he returns to the mother of all the living,
> His thoughts, the fear in his heart,
>> and his troubled forebodings till the day he dies —
> Whether he sits on a lofty throne
>> or grovels in dust and ashes,
> Whether he bears a splendid crown
>> or is wrapped in the coarsest of cloaks —
> Are of wrath and envy, trouble and dread,
>> terror of death, fury and strife.
> Even when he lies on his bed to rest,
>> his cares at night disturb his sleep (40:1–5).

Sirach's resignation in all this is not that of a weakling. His expression of human woes indicates how deeply he feels them. It is a triumph of his faith in God that he can submit to a pattern that he can neither understand nor control.

These passages need to be balanced by other views of Sirach before we have the complete picture of his philosophy of life. It still remains true that, for him, happiness is also possible in this life. Primarily, he sought it in wisdom, fear of the Lord, good living. We have already seen some of the ingredients of his concept of happiness: "Happy the husband of a good wife" (26:1); "More precious than gold is health and well-being" (30:15); "Happy the man who meditates on wisdom" (14:20), and these generalities could be multiplied; they show the broad, balanced judgment of a man who knows the world — and God. Yet, we may ask, what was Sirach really like? Can we break through these generalities to appreciate the human struggle that marked his life? There are some indications of this aspect of the man. It would be a mistake to think that his faith and resignation were an easy achievement:

> My son, from your youth embrace discipline;
> thus will you find wisdom with graying hair.
> As though plowing and sowing, draw close to her;
> then await her bountiful crops.
> For in cultivating her you will labor but little,
> and soon you will eat of her fruits.
> How irksome she is to the unruly!
> The fool cannot abide her.
> She will be like a burdensome stone to test him,
> and he will not delay in casting her aside.
> For discipline is like her name,
> she is not accessible to [i.e., disciplined by] many
>
> (6:18–23).

One feels that the attainment of Sirach's wisdom was more than "little labor," that he is playing down his own efforts in view of the goal he has reached. The following passage tells us the kind of man he was, better perhaps than the encomium he heaps upon the pursuit of wisdom:

Be ashamed of hostility toward the people where you settle,
   and of conflict with him who pitches his tent beside you;
Of refusing to give when asked,
   of defrauding another of his appointed share,
Of failing to return a greeting,
   and of rebuffing a friend;
Of lusting after another's wife,
   and of trifling with his maid;
Of using harsh words with friends,
   and of accompanying your gifts with insults;
Of repeating what you hear,
   and of betraying secrets —
These are the things that you should rightly avoid as shameful
   if you would be looked upon by everyone with favor

(41:18–24).

It would be shortsighted for us to emphasize the motive given in
41:24. It is rather the result, yearned for and appreciated, it is
true, of the difficult and noble morality of Sirach.

But with this Spartan attitude (cf. 51:18–20 quoted above)
went a cheerful delight in the little pleasures of this world. Sirach
was not the ascetic type:

When wine is present, do not pour out discourse,
   and flaunt not your wisdom at the wrong time.
Like a seal of carnelian in a setting of gold
   is a concert when wine is served.
Like a gold mounting with an emerald seal
   is string music with delicious wine (32:4–6).

Wine is very life to man
   if taken in moderation.
Does he really live who lacks the wine
   which was created for his joy?
Joy of heart, good cheer and merriment
   are wine drunk freely at the proper time (31:27 f.).

There is a certain accent of Coheleth in this; the little pleasures
that life affords are to be enjoyed. And it is consoling that this is

recognized by a man so dedicated to wisdom. He deserves to be counted among the wise whom he neatly describes:

A man may be wise and benefit many,
  yet be of no use to himself.
Though a man be wise, if his words are rejected
  he will be deprived of all enjoyment.
When a man is wise to his own advantage,
  the fruits of his knowledge are seen in his own person;
When a man is wise to his people's advantage,
  the fruits of his knowledge are enduring.
Limited are the days of one man's life,
  but the life of Israel is days without number (37:19–23).

Riches and Poverty

Sirach makes it clear that the vocation of a scribe is possible only for those who have leisure (38:24 ff.), and presumably he was a man of comfortable means. His reference to his travels (34:11), to servants (33:25–33), to conduct before people of influence (8:1 f.; 13:4–13), and to banquets (31:12–32:13) all confirm this impression of a bourgeois scribe. In the light of this background, his attitude towards material possessions is all the more interesting.

Like all the wisdom writers, he ever insists on diligence:

My son, hold fast to your duty, busy yourself with it,
  grow old while doing your task (11:20).

Hence he has no sympathy with a poverty that results from laziness:

My son, live not the life of a beggar,
  better to die than to beg (40:28; cf. 22:1 f.).

But his attitude toward the poor is most commendable, and it is motivated by religious considerations:

To a poor man, however, be generous;
  keep him not waiting for your alms;
Because of the precept, help the needy,
  and in their want do not send them away empty-handed.

> Spend your money for your brother and friend,
>   and hide it not under a stone to perish;
> Dispose of your treasure as the Most High commands,
>   for that will profit you more than the gold (29:8–11).

The poor are to be given a hearing and their greeting courteously returned (4:5). The outward appearance is not the true test of a man:

> Mock not the worn cloak
>   and jibe at no man's bitter day:
> For strange are the works of the Lord,
>   hidden from men his deeds (11:4).

It is the proud rich who abhor the poor (13:19). Sirach's sympathies are clearly with the poor, and his careful and cautious attitude toward the rich confirms this:

> Contend not with an influential man,
>   lest you fall into his power.
> Quarrel not with a rich man,
>   lest he pay out the price of your downfall;
> For gold has dazzled many,
>   and perverts the character of princes (8:1 f.).

If he himself never experienced such maltreatment (but cf. 51:2–5), he seems to have witnessed it and always remained wary of the rich. With his characteristic clarity of thought, he also recognized the difference money makes and has expressed this truth in the following observations:

> Honored in poverty, how much more so in wealth!
>   Dishonored in wealth, in poverty how much the more!
> $\qquad\qquad\qquad\qquad\qquad\qquad$ (10:30.)

> The rich man does wrong and boast of it,
>   the poor man is wronged and begs forgiveness (13:3).

> A rich man speaks and all are silent,
>   his wisdom they extol to the clouds.
> A poor man speaks and they say: "Who is that?"
>   If he slips they cast him down (13:22).

As Coheleth had observed, money answers for everything (10:19). Nonetheless, Sirach was able to recognize that money is at the root of evil:

> The lover of gold will not be free from sin,
>> for he who pursues wealth is led astray by it.
>
> Many have been ensnared by gold,
>> though destruction lay before their eyes;
>
> It is a stumbling block to those who are avid for it,
>> a snare for every fool (31:5–7).

> Wealth is good when there is no sin;
>> but poverty is evil by the standards of the proud (13:23).

He is able to keep a very balanced judgment on riches and the enjoyment of earthly pleasures. On the one hand, they are there to be enjoyed:

> Deprive not yourself of present good things,
>> let no choice portion escape you . . .
>
> Give, take, and treat yourself well,
>> for in the nether world there are no joys to seek (14:14 ff.).

But on the other hand,

> To the poor man also extend your hand,
>> that your blessing may be complete;
>
> Be generous to all the living,
>> and withhold not your kindness from the dead (7:32 f.).

Women and Marriage

In discussing the Canticle of Canticles we quoted in a rather one-sided manner a judgment which Sirach made upon a wicked woman (25:12–17). Although there are many other passages which might appear harsh (25:18–25; 9:1–9; 26:5–12), the following offer a certain needed balance in order to obtain a correct idea of Sirach's views:

Happy the husband of a good wife,
  twice-lengthened are his days;
A worthy wife brings joy to her husband,
  peaceful and full is his life.
A good wife is a generous gift
  bestowed upon him who fears the Lord;
Be he rich or poor, his heart is content,
  and a smile is ever on his face (26:1–4).

Choicest of blessings is a modest wife,
  priceless her chaste person.
Like the sun rising in the Lord's heavens,
  the beauty of a virtuous wife is the radiance of her home.
Like the light which shines above the holy lampstand,
  are her beauty of face and graceful figure.
Golden columns on silver bases
  are her shapely limbs and steady feet (26:15–18).

Both of these descriptions show that the ideal wife of Proverbs 31 was very much alive in the Hebrew tradition. But in almost every discussion of wifely virtue the primary consideration is the happiness that a good wife brings to the *man*. The woman of a different background, such as that of today, might with reason say that little value is placed on woman as a person in the Old Testament; in short, this is a man's world.

Typical of this superior male attitude is 36:21:

Though any man may be accepted as a husband,
  yet one girl will be more suitable than another.

The choice of a partner in marriage belongs only to the male. Moreover, it is always the woman who is described as seductive and leading man to sin. It is she who needs constant supervision:

A daughter is a treasure that keeps her father wakeful,
  and worry over her drives away rest:
Lest she pass her prime unmarried,
  or when she is married, lest she be repudiated;
While unmarried, lest she be seduced,
  or, as a wife, lest she prove unfaithful;

Lest she conceive in her father's house,
 or be sterile in that of her husband.
Keep a close watch on your daughter,
 lest she make you the sport of your enemies,
A byword in the city, a reproach among the people,
 an object of derision in public gatherings.
See that there is no lattice in her room,
 no place that overlooks the approaches to the house
(42:9–11).

How are we to view this Old Testament attitude toward women? Is this a theologoumenon, an inspired "teaching" which is to be considered an expression of God's will and revelation? By no means. It has no more validity than the polygamy which was practiced in the Old Testament days. It is an expression, not of God's will, but of the *mores* of the time in which these writers lived. Today, due to the influence of the Christian tradition, we judge such an attitude toward woman as unenlightened and imperfect. No other verdict seems possible. But one can be grateful that the appearance of a Jewess, Mary, has contributed greatly to the changing of this point of view.

The Praise of the Fathers

In a departure from the usual wisdom theme, Sirach here has recourse to history, to the sacred history of his own people. Nowhere before have we seen a treatment of Israel's history as part of wisdom. Even Proverbs 1–9, which depends so much upon the writing prophets (Isaias and Jeremias) and upon Deuteronomy, is content to remain within the usual didactic framework. But perhaps we can understand why Sirach should now include Israelite history in his teaching. As we have already noted, he identified wisdom with the Law of Moses. This identification suggests a strongly nationalistic attitude toward wisdom, in contrast to the earlier, somewhat more universal attitude (recall that even Job was a non-Israelite). The next logical step would be to exemplify wisdom in the lives of outstanding Israelites who had lived under this Law. Sirach is not alone in thus concretizing wisdom in examples from history. The didactic psalm 78 is similar in that it draws a lesson from Israel's history, but without giving a list of heroes. The author of the book of Wisdom, as we shall see, has dedicated a large section to history to show what Wisdom achieved through her followers (cc. 10–12; 16–19). In the New Testament the eleventh chapter of the Epistle to the Hebrews is similar in purpose.

The incipient threat of the Hellenistic way of life is doubtless another factor which prompted Sirach to turn to his own national resources and to offer them to his people. He would overlook no means to make their sacred traditions attractive to a "new" generation that could be seduced by the dazzling achievements of Greece. This aspect of his polemic is somewhat subtle, for there is no explicit reference to Hellenism. But the past glories are described not so much for their own sake as for the practical lesson they have for Sirach's contemporaries. We may point to his treatment of Enoch, Noe, and Abraham as examples of his apologetic interest.

This section of Sirach's book takes its title from 44:1, "Now will I praise these godly men, our fathers." The praise of the fathers is really subordinate to the praise of God which Sirach begins in 42:15, so that it forms the major part of a large poem concerned with the glory of God (42:15–50:24). The first part (42:15–43:35) describes "God's works," his wonders in the world he created; the rest (44:1–50:24) is taken up with the men whose lives have been fashioned "according to his will" (50:22). Within the Praise of the Fathers the following division is indicated:

> 44:1–15, introduction
> 44:16–49:13, Enoch to Nehemias
> 49:14–16, Enoch back to Adam
> 50:1–24, Simon, High-Priest in Sirach's time

The apologetic bent of this review of Israel's history appears in the list of over twenty personages who are discussed. The notice concerning Enoch, who is mentioned twice (44:16; 49:14), is restrained in comparison to the contemporary traditions that had formed around him. In the apocryphal *Book of Jubilees*, his "assumption" to God is described with a wealth of detail. As a seer who knows past and future, he is a champion of whom Hebrew tradition could boast; his knowledge far surpassed Greek culture. Sirach praises him for his being taken up to God; there could be no greater recognition than this. Sirach then turns to Noe, "found just and perfect" among a sinful generation. This reference can easily have overtones reflecting on the wickedness of the Hellenistic world in which Sirach lived. Speaking of Abraham (44:19 ff.), he highlights his loyalty to the covenant and promise of God, for in Sirach's day fidelity to the covenant and Jewish tradition was being tested. He goes on through Moses, Josue, and the rest of the "redemption-history" of Israel. Naturally David and Solomon, the latter not without blame for the folly of his old age, are discussed in detail. But the longest descriptions are reserved for Aaron the first High Priest, and Simon, son of Jonathan, whose officiating Sirach himself had witnessed. His enthusiasm for the priesthood knows no bounds. Of Simon he says:

> How splendid he was as he appeared from the Tent,
> as he came from within the veil!
> Like a star shining among the clouds,
> like the full moon at the holyday season;
> Like the sun shining upon the temple,
> like the rainbow appearing in the cloudy sky (50:5–7).

In 50:12–21 he has left a touching picture of religious festival in Jerusalem about 200 B.C.

These are only a few examples chosen by Sirach as exemplars of what God wrought through Israel. He closes the list with a prayer:

> May his goodness toward us endure in Israel
> as long as the heavens are above (50:24).

The force of these great heroes was not to be lost on his readers. When Sirach wrote (of the prophets, 49:10) "May their bones return to life," he wanted to see a renewal and revitalization of traditional religious practice among his people — and it came about in the Maccabean revolt.

Conclusion

Of all the sapiential books, Sirach is perhaps least appreciated. His remarks do not have the pungency of most of the Proverbs; he is far from being the equal of the poet who wrote Job; he lacks the insight of Coheleth. He seems reactionary in comparison to the new ideas about a blessed immortality which the author of Wisdom puts forth. Yet he has an earnestness and charm which will win many readers. But it seems almost fatal for a beginner to read the book from start to finish. It is suggested that the following selections will be a help to the prospective reader. Sirach, as was pointed out above, follows no particular order; hence this outline puts together (with only slight overlapping) the main topics which he discusses:

1. Autobiographical references:
    prologue; 50:25-29; 51; 38:24-39:11 (his vocation — wisdom); see also 6:18-37; 14:20-15:10; 24; 34:9-13; 33:16-18.
2. Friends and friendship:
    6:5-17; 9:10-16; 11:29-34; 12:1-18; 13:1-25; 22:19-26; 26:19-27:21; 36:18-37:15.
3. Speech:
    5:11-6:1; 19:5-16; 20:17-28; 23:7-15; 27:4-15; 28:12-26.
4. Providence:
    2:1-11; 11:10-28; 15:11-20; 16:1-17:27, 18:1-13; 32:14-33:18; 35:10-24.
5. Praise of the Fathers:
    44:1-50:24.
6. Woman and marriage:
    9:1-9; 25:1-26:18; 36:21-27; 42:9-14.
7. Miscellany:
    3:17-28; 4:20-31; 7:18-36; 10:6-30; 20:1-16; 22:27-23:6; 31:12-32:13; 34:18-35:24; 36:1-17; 38:1-23; 39:12-35; cc. 40-43.

8. JEWISH WISDOM IN A GREEK WORLD

IN THE very first verse of the book of Wisdom we meet a problem that is not easy to solve: Why did the pseudo-Solomon address himself to "you who judge the earth," that is, kings? It is easy enough to understand why our unknown author assumed the *nom de plume* of King Solomon. Solomon was the great Jewish king of the gloried past, and a patron of wisdom. Coheleth had also assumed Solomon's authority. But Coheleth had never lectured pagan kings, as this author does. Moreover, although the book is addressed by Solomon to his colleagues, it is also unmistakably aimed at his fellow Jews in the great capital city of Alexandria, who are threatened by the surrounding paganism. This is an intensely Jewish book, despite the inevitable influence which Greek thought exercised upon the author. Although he wrote in Greek, he employs Old Testament thoughts and phrases throughout, in the manner of *style anthologique*, discussed above in the case of Sirach. His most distinctive contribution, the doctrine of blessed immortality, is arrived at and expressed in a typically Jewish manner. But ostensibly he addresses himself to pagan colleagues. Why?

For one thing, we are still within the ambit of wisdom literature, whose origins have been located in court life — Egyptian and Israelite. It should not be too surprising to find a wisdom treatise directed to kings; even Coheleth's writing contained several statements about royalty. Second, the Jews felt that they were kings. After all, wisdom was a Jewish possession and it was royal: "the desire for Wisdom leads up to a kingdom" (Wis 6:20), and wisdom showed Jacob "the kingdom of God" (10:10). Hence it appears that the address to the kings of the earth in 1:1 and 6:1-2 is more than just a literary device; the message is for the true kings, the

Jews themselves. Finally, the writer is following an established tradition, found in earlier biblical writings, of addressing a wide audience. The book of Isaias begins "Hear, O heavens, and listen, O earth!" (1:2). Osee (5:1) and Micheas (3:1, 9) call out to rulers. Psalm 2:10, 12 (in the Septuagint translation the relation to Wisdom 1:1; 6:1 ff. is even clearer) carries an admonition to the "judges of the earth" to be wise and keep from injustice. The "invitation to learning" given by the author of Wisdom follows this pattern.

Typically enough, the author has derived his address to the kings in 6:1 f. from Isaias 51:4 in the ancient Greek translation (Septuagint) which he knew so well:

> Listen to me, listen to me, O my people!
> O kings, give ear to me!

The interesting fact is that the original reading, found in the Hebrew text, had "O my nation," instead of "O kings" but the author adopts the Septuagint reading which makes kings of the Israelites. After the initial address (1:1), the author takes up the theme of immortality in chapters 1–5, but he returns to the theme of kingship and wisdom in chapters 6–9:

> Hear, therefore, kings, and understand;
>   learn, you magistrates of the earth's expanse!
> Hearken, you who rule the multitude
>   and lord it over throngs of peoples!
> Because authority was given you by the Lord
>   and sovereignty by the Most High,
>   who shall probe your works and scrutinize your counsels!
>
> (6:1–3.)

> To you, therefore, O princes, are my words addressed
>   that you may learn wisdom and that you may not sin.
> For those who keep the holy precepts hallowed shall be found
>   holy
>   and those learned in them will have ready a response.
> Desire therefore my words;
>   long for them and you shall be instructed.

Resplendent and unfading is Wisdom,
    and she is readily perceived by those who love her,
    and found by those who seek her (6:9–12).

If, then, you find pleasure in throne and scepter, you princes
    of the peoples,
    honor Wisdom, that you may reign forever (6:21).

This doctrine is reflected in other parts of the book. It is wisdom
that brought Joseph "the scepter of royalty" (10:14). It was
wisdom that Solomon loved:

Her I loved and sought after from my youth;
    I sought to take her for my bride
    and was enamored of her beauty.
She adds to nobility the splendor of companionship with
    God;
    even the Lord of all loved her (8:2–3).

As against the divinization of royalty, Solomon stresses that he is
but "a mortal man, like all the rest":

And I too, when born, inhaled the common air,
    and fell upon the kindred earth;
    wailing, I uttered that first sound common to all.
In swaddling clothes and with constant care I was nurtured,
For no king has any different origin or birth,
    but one is the entry into life for all; and in one same way
    they leave it (7:3–6).

Hence he had to pray for wisdom:

Therefore I prayed, and prudence was given me;
    I pleaded, and the spirit of Wisdom came to me.
I preferred her to scepter and throne,
    and deemed riches nothing in comparison with her
                                   (7:7–8).

This prayer is reflected in the beautiful words of chapter 9, which
is not unlike the prayer of Solomon at Gabaon in 3 Kings 8:15–61.

God of my fathers, Lord of mercy,
  you who have made all things by your word
And in your wisdom have established man
  to rule the creatures produced by you,
To govern the world in holiness and justice,
  and to render judgment in integrity of heart:
Give me Wisdom, the attendant at your throne,
  and reject me not from among your children . . . (9:1–4).

Send her forth from your holy heavens
  and from your glorious throne dispatch her
That she may be with me and work with me,
  that I may know what is pleasing to you.
For she knows and understands all things,
  and will guide me discreetly in my affairs
  and safeguard me by her glory . . . (9:10–11).

The long description of wisdom prepares the way for the development of her activity from Adam to the Hebrew exodus (10:1–21), and God's special Providence over his people in the exodus itself (11:2–12:27; 15:18–19:22).

Midrashic History (10:1–21; 11:2–12:27; 15:18–19:22)

Pseudo-Solomon's treatment of the redemptive history of the Jews is an example of the literary genre of midrash. This is a devotional, edifying, interpretation of historical events in order to point up moral or spiritual lessons. It might be compared to the homiletic approach of a modern preacher who analyzes a biblical episode in order to adapt it to the spiritual needs of his audience. Such an analysis is not designed to be definitive or historical; a certain liberty and even artificiality are allowed in order to make a point. This is obvious in the procedure followed by pseudo-Solomon: he submits seven items of the exodus story to minute analysis and contrast.

I (11:2–14). The water with which God supplied the Jews from the rock stands in contrast to the thirst which afflicted the Egyptians in the first plague, the bloody Nile: "For by the things through which their foes were punished they in their need were benefited" (11:5). In the contrasting treatment of Jews and Egyptians we see the author of Wisdom 1–5 at work. The Jews are like the just man of the first chapters; the Egyptians are the wicked. The former are only mildly chastised (11:9; cf. 3:5; 4:10 ff.), while the latter are tormented.

II (11:15–12:27 & 15:18–16:14). The animals (frogs, flies, gnats, locusts) which punished the Egyptians in the series of plagues are contrasted with the quail with which God fed Israel. The author finds many lessons in God's punitive use of animals:

> . . . that they might recognize that a man is punished
>   by the very things through which he sins
>   (11:15; cf. 12:27).

Egyptian deities were represented in animal form; one need only recall the attacks of Herodotus, Cicero, and Juvenal on Egyptian worship of the crocodile, the ibis, fish, cats, etc. Thus the Egyptians "were tortured by the very things they deemed gods" (12:27). The writer hastens to add that God could have destroyed this people at once with powerful animals or a single blast by his mighty spirit. But he did not do this because he *loves* all things that exist. Rather, he was giving the wicked time to repent:

> Therefore you rebuke offenders little by little,
>   warn them, and remind them of the sins they are
>   committing,
>   that they may abandon their wickedness and believe in
>   you, O Lord! (12:2)

This same mercy and wisdom is instanced in the history of the Canaanites (12:3–22). Here again God could have wiped them out by battle, beasts, "or by one decisive word" (12:9). But in exterminating them slowly he gave them time to repent:

> And you taught your people, by these deeds,
>   that those who are just must be kind;
> And you gave your sons good ground for hope
>   that you would permit repentance for their sins.

For these were enemies of your servants, doomed to death;
yet, while you punished them with such solicitude and
pleading,
granting time and opportunity to abandon wickedness,
With what exactitude you judged your sons,
to whose fathers you gave the sworn covenants of goodly
promises!
Us, therefore, you chastise, and our enemies with a thousand
blows you punish,
that we may think earnestly of your goodness when we
judge,
and, when being judged, may look for mercy (12:19–22).

III (16:5–15). Although the Egyptians were bitten by the
locusts and flies and had no remedy, the Hebrews were saved from
the fiery serpents by the "sign of salvation," the bronze serpent.
As though uncomfortably aware of the worship reputedly given to
this image in Israel's history (4 Kgs 18:4), the writer emphasizes
that whoever turned to the bronze serpent "was saved, not by what
he saw, but by you, the savior of all" (16:7).

IV (16:15–29). Rain, hailstorms and fire (i.e., lightning) combined in a miraculous manner to punish the Egyptians. The fire
and water were each tempered so that they did not cancel each
other out, but could do their work of destruction: "for the universe
fights on behalf of the just" (16:17). On the other hand, what was
poured down from heaven upon Israel? Manna, "the bread from
heaven, ready to hand, untoiled-for, endowed with all delights
and conforming to every taste" (16:20). Here, too, the elements
were tempered:

Yet snow and ice withstood fire and were not melted,
that they might know that their enemies' fruits
Were consumed by a fire that blazed in the hail
and flashed lightning in the rain (16:22).

The author indicates by this that the manna was actually baked
by the Jews (the "snow and ice" withstood fire), although the rays
of the sun were sufficient to melt it. There are lessons for the Jews
to learn:

For your creation, serving you, its maker,
    grows tense for punishment against the wicked,
    but is relaxed in benefit for those who trust in you (16:24).

The action of the sun on the manna is also explained:

So that men might know that one must give you thanks before
        the sunrise,
    and turn to you at daybreak (16:28).

V (17:1–18:4). The darkness of the ninth plague filled the
Egyptians with terror, and the writer has a vivid imaginative description of the terrors of darkness in 17:3–7, 18–19. In contrast,
the Jews had the pillar of fire. The observations made about wickedness and fear in this connection are worth quoting:

For wickedness, of its nature cowardly, testifies in its own
        condemnation,
    and because of a distressed conscience, always magnifies
        misfortunes.
For fear is nought but the surrender of the helps that come
        from reason;
    and the more one's expectation is of itself uncertain,
    the more one makes of not knowing the cause that brings
        on torment (17:11–13).

After all, it was only just that the Jews "through whom the im-
perishable light of the Law was to be given to the world" (18:4),
should have enjoyed God's light.

VI (18:5–19:4). Egypt's first-born were slain by God's "all-
powerful word from heaven's royal throne" (18:15). By contrast,
the Israelites were delivered from the plague at Cades through the
intercession of Aaron.

VII (19:5). The Egyptians drowned in the Red Sea while the
Jews crossed safely.

This homiletic treatment of the exodus story is followed by a
conclusion (19:6–19) which more or less summarizes the many
marvelous features of this story: fire, water, all creation combined
to save God's people, for God "stood by them in every time and

circumstance" (19:22). One final word: The approach of pseudo-Solomon to the redemptive history may strike us as artificial and contrived. That is because we as Christians look rather too soberly upon this history. Yet the writer's method of interpretation might be compared to the legendary accounts with which Christian devotion has surrounded the story of Christ's life. Just as devout imagination has been at work on the fourteen stations of the "way of the Cross" in an effort to appropriate and apply the mystery of the Redemption, so pseudo-Solomon worked with his sacred history.

Idolatry (13:1–15:17)

We may find ourselves even more out of sympathy with the author's treatment of idolatry. His method of argumentation is not particularly convincing to us. He adopts an irony that is often heavy-handed (13:16 f.). He creates imaginary situations from which idolatry arose, and then has no difficulty in ridiculing the straw men which he sets up (14:15 ff.). In this he is imitating a type of literature that became prevalent after the exile (539), and is exemplified in Is 44:9 ff.; Jer 10:1–16, and in the so-called letter of Jeremias (the sixth chapter of the book of Baruch). The same ridicule is expressed perhaps more successfully in story form in the tale of Bel and the dragon which is appended to the book of Daniel (Dn 14).

The reason that moderns are less impressed with this manner of argumentation is that we refuse to believe that such a crass mentality existed. Idolators did not worship the wood; it was merely an image of a god, or in some way inhabited by a god. Hence we feel that the author is missing the mark when he writes as if idolators identified an image as a god. That is our privilege, which fits our logical approach to a situation. But the approach of this type of literature is not that of a logical treatise; it is a form of satire rather than argumentation, and must be judged from that point of view. It creates a mentality against idols which is all the writer wishes to achieve. Moreover, there is a certain dialectic in the author's argument. The "other gods" have been shown up throughout Israel's history as impotent, as "nothings." They cannot act, therefore they do not exist. Thus Deutero-Isaias can challenge them:

> Do something, good or evil,
>   that we all may look on in wonderment.
> Why, you are nothing, and your work is nought! (Is 41:23 f.)

Since the gods do not exist, to what is the worship of an idolator directed? Obviously, only to the wooden image which alone remains.

The author's first point (13:1–9) is well taken. It is a condemnation of nature worship or the worship of any created thing. A thinker should be able to rise above what is made, no matter its beauty, to the one who made it. The author is not presenting an argument for the existence of God after the manner of the "Five Ways" of St. Thomas. As a genuine Hebrew he does not even conceive of the pure atheist. That God exists is a fact — but who and what is he? It is here that some men go wrong, identifying him with elements or stars. "For these the blame is less," but they cannot be pardoned:

> For if they so far succeeded in knowledge
>   that they could speculate about the world,
>   how did they not more quickly find its Lord? (13:9.)

But those who earn the author's condemnation and scorn are the idolators or image worshipers. And we have the imagined case of a carpenter who uses the rejected wood for the image carved "to occupy his spare time" (13:13). This painted image must be fastened in a shrine lest it fall; it can give no answer to requests. Wood has served many good purposes and Noe's ark is praised as "the wood through which justice is fulfilled" (14:7). How did idolatry originate? The author presents three sources: mourning for a dead child led to the image of him which is venerated (ancestor worship?); the desire to have images of an absent king; the ambition of artists (cf. Horace in *Satires* I:8, 1–3). The result is moral chaos, which is described in a powerful passage:

And all is confusion — blood and murder, theft and guile,
   corruption, faithlessness, turmoil, perjury,
Disturbance of good men, neglect of gratitude,
   besmirching of souls, unnatural lust,
   disorder in marriage, adultery and shamelessness.
For the worship of infamous idols
   is the reason and source and extremity of all evil
                                                   (14:25–27).

Blessed Immortality (1:1–5:23)

It is difficult for a Christian to grasp the fact that the Hebrews
lived without any belief in a future life of reward or punishment.
In the discussion of Job and Coheleth we have seen something of
the Hebrew ideas on Sheol, or the nether world. We also saw that
this limitation is characteristic of the largest part of Old Testament
literature, except for the rare break-throughs noted for the Psalms
(16??, 49, 73), and for Isaias 26:19 and Daniel 12:2 f. It is often
asserted that the logic of Old Testament thought postulated the
resurrection of the body as expressed in the book of Daniel and
which seems to be a common belief during the days of the
Maccabees (2 Mc 7:9 ff.; 14:46). This is quite true. Since man,
according to the Hebrews, is a unit and not a composite of body
and soul, he stands or falls with his body. However, this "reason"
is no more than our own logical reconstruction; such a speculative
approach to the *manner* of living after death is totally absent from
Israelite thought. By the same token, there was never any speculation as to "what" was in Sheol; they were "shades" (*r⁰pha'im*)
but never further specified. This total lack of speculation enabled
the Israelites to speak of people in the nether world, after they
were buried on earth, without saying either that it was an "immortal soul" which remained in existence. This is the heart of the
matter: speculation or theoretical analysis concerning the nature
of man after death simply does not exist. Man went to Sheol, and
imagination takes over to describe his bleak existence there.
   This freedom from the necessity of any philosophical justification of their position aligned the Jewish approach to immortality

in the direction of *union with God*. The most acute expression of
this approach is Ps 73:23–28:

> Yet with you I shall always be;
>   you have hold of my right hand;
> With your counsel you guide me,
>   and in the end you will receive me in glory.
> Whom else have I in heaven?
>   And when I am with you, the earth delights me not.
> Though my flesh and my heart waste away,
>   God is the rock of my heart and my portion forever.
> For indeed, they who withdraw from you perish;
>   you destroy everyone who is unfaithful to you.
> But for me, to be near God is my good;
>   to make the Lord God my refuge.
> I shall declare all your works
>   in the gates of the daughter of Sion.

The mind of the psalmist is that here is a union which simply
perdures. Again, there is no thought as to the manner in which
this will be achieved; this union continues. Nor is it licit to conclude that the psalmist envisioned the resurrection of the body
since that was more "logical" for him than the concept of the
immortality of the soul. He says nothing about either, and logic
is irrelevant here.

These preliminary remarks are necessary in view of the extreme interpretations of the book of Wisdom. Exegetes have favored
two views: the Wisdom writer speaks of bodily resurrection or else
the immortality of the soul (naturally, this last under the influence
of Greek thought). We think there is a middle position: We do
not think that the author of Wisdom says anything about the
manner (in the body or out of the body) in which man will enjoy
immortality. There is only the fact that man is immortal and the
only reason given to support this fact is *union with God* (justice),
or specifically, association with the sons of God in the next life.

The author's ideas on the future life are revealed almost at
once. In the first chapter, one feels that he is using the terms life
and death in a far more pregnant sense than is common among the

wisdom writers. Death includes spiritual death in the sense of sin, and (eternal) separation from God, while life embraces the notion of union with God:

> Court not death by your erring way of life,
>> nor draw to yourselves destruction by the works of your hands.
> Because God did not make death,
>> nor does he rejoice in the destruction of the living.
> For he fashioned all things that they might have being;
>> and the creatures of the world are wholesome,
> And there is not a destructive drug among them
>> nor any domain of the nether world on earth,
>> for justice is immortal.
> It was the wicked who with hands and words invited death,
>> considered it a friend and pined for it;
> They made a covenant with it,
>> because they deserve to be in its possession (1:12–16).

The only adequate understanding of this text must recognize that the word "death" here has overtones; it goes beyond the end of merely physical existence, because death is associated with the wicked: they covenant with it and are possessed by it. This could not be merely physical death, which claims the just as well as the wicked. The meaning of death includes sin or separation from God. God himself made man for life, as the author will say in 2:23 f.:

> For God formed man to be imperishable;
>> the image of his own nature he made him.
> But by the envy of the devil, death entered the world,
>> and they who are in his possession experience it.

While this is an obvious reference to man's loss of physical immortality in the Paradise story of Genesis 2 f., the statement of verse 24 clearly implies that the death experienced by those on the side of the devil involves separation from God. Since the just "die," what does their death mean? The author tells us that they do not really die; physical death means nothing because "justice is immortal."

After a lively description of the wicked, their views on life, and their reaction to the just man whom they persecute unto death (2:1–20), the author returns to the theme of immortality:

> But the souls of the just are in the hand of God,
>> and no torment shall touch them.
> They seemed, in the view of the foolish, to be dead;
>> and their passing away was judged an affliction
>> and their going forth from us, utter destruction.
> But they are in peace (3:1–3).

While the phrase "in the hand of God" was used by Job (12:10) and Coheleth (9:1), it has a deeper sense here, equivalent to "peace." Death is not really death for the just (3:2). As the words of the Requiem Mass put it, "life is changed, not taken away."

What about the suffering of the just man, the problem that so exercised Jeremias, Job, and Coheleth? No philosophical answer is given; their suffering was a trial which proved them:

> Chastised a little, they shall be greatly blessed,
>> because God tried them
>> and found them worthy of himself.
> As gold in the furnace, he proved them,
>> and as sacrificial offerings he took them to himself (3:5 f.).

The description of their condition is expressed in the beautiful lines:

> Those who trust in him shall understand truth,
>> and the faithful shall abide with him in love:
>> because grace and mercy are with his chosen ones (3:9).

The otherworldly viewpoint of the author is somewhat interrupted by the this-worldly viewpoint on retribution in 3:10–4:4. It is at first surprising to find the author attempting to solve the problems of this life by the traditional theory. He feels compelled to offer the maximum consolation to the distressed and the oppressed even in this life. Hence he enunciates a typical traditional principle:

> For he who despises wisdom and instruction is doomed.
> Vain is their hope, fruitless are their labors,
> > and worthless are their works (3:11).

However, there is a significant reversal of values in the application of the theory. Traditionally, the childless was one struck by God; the eunuch was one who was cut off from the community of Israel (Dt 23:2). The author singles out these afflicted as examples of people who are in fact *blessed*, if they are just. Because their justice will entitle them to immortality. What about the just man who dies early, who is not rewarded with a long life on earth as the traditional theory demands (4:7–16)? The author reverses the time-honored judgment on gray hair:

> For the age that is honorable comes not with the passing of
> > time,
> > nor can it be measured in terms of years.
> Rather, understanding is the hoary crown for men,
> > and an unsullied life, the attainment of old age (4:8–9).

Virtue counts, not a long life. And when a good man dies young, this is part of God's plan:

> He who pleased God was loved;
> > he who lived among sinners was transported —
> Snatched away, lest wickedness pervert his mind
> > or deceit beguile his soul; . . .
> Having become perfect in a short while, he reached the
> > fullness of a long career;
> > for his soul was pleasing to the Lord,
> > therefore he sped him out of the midst of wickedness
> > > (4:10 f., 13 f.).

On the other hand, the wicked become "dishonored corpses," "utterly laid waste," and they "shall be in grief." This is as much as he says about any punishment of the evil in the next world — grief.

The scene of the Final Judgment (4:20–5:23) is quite imaginative. As the just man confronts his oppressors, the latter are shocked, and they cry out acknowledging the fate of the just.

They shall say among themselves, rueful,
  and groaning through anguish of spirit:
"This is he whom once we held as a laughingstock
  and as a type for mockery, fools that we were!
His life we deemed madness,
  and his death dishonored.
See how he is accounted among the sons of God;
  how his lot is with the saints!" (5:3–5.)

In this last verse we return to the manner in which the author of
Wisdom envisioned survival in the next life. Man's reward is
described as an association with the sons of God, the "holy ones,"
or angels. This is the bridge by which the author crosses the line
of death. There is a remarkable parallelism in thought between
this approach of the book of Wisdom and the thought of the
Essenes of Qumran. Their "Manual of Discipline," discovered
among the so-called Dead Sea Scrolls in Cave 1 in 1947, describes
the state of their members in these words:

Those whom God has chosen he has made an eternal possession,
an inheritance in the lot of the holy ones, and he has united
their assembly with the sons of heaven — to be the congregation
of the community, the assembly of a holy building, an eternal
planting for all time. (1QS 11:7–8; see also 1QH 3:20–22.)

It is not clear whether this association with the holy ones is conceived by the people of Qumran as being in the next life or only
in this life; the former assumption seems probable. But there can
be no question about the book of Wisdom. Association with the
sons of God, the "lot" with the saints, is clearly envisioned after
death. And it is within this framework that the author concludes
to immortality. He makes no use of the idea of the soul's imma-
teriality or natural immortality (even if Wis 9:15 suggests that he
is aware of it), or of the final resurrection of the body.

This final beatitude of man is further developed in 5:5 f.:

But the just live forever,
  and in the Lord is their recompense,
  and the thought of them is with the Most High.

> Therefore shall they receive the splendid crown,
>   the beauteous diadem, from the hand of the Lord —
> For he shall shelter them with his right hand,
>   and protect them with his arm.

The reward of the just is described in terms derived from Is 62:3. These are merely metaphorical and should not be pressed so hard as to imply a bodily resurrection.

Thus, when Old Testament thought finally broke through into the clear light of blessed immortality, it did so in its own way. An eternal life with God was, as it were, "demanded" by Jewish thought. The God whom they knew was too great, too merciful, to allow his faithful to be herded into Sheol; they were to remain united with him. The author indicates this trend:

> But you, our God, are good and true,
>   slow to anger, and governing all with mercy.
> For even if we sin, we are yours, and know your might;
>   but we will not sin, knowing that we belong to you.
> For to know you well is complete justice,
>   and to know your might is the root of immortality
>   (15:1-3).

The similarity of this to St. John's words (17:3) is evident: "For this is eternal life, that they may know thee, the one true God, and Jesus Christ, whom thou hast sent." There is a definite similarity between the Jewish and Christian approach. Union with God leads to association with his holy ones forever (justice is immortal); for the Christian, the union with God in this life through the grace of Christ flowers into the beatific vision of God in the next — "for this is eternal life. . . ."

9. WISDOM IN THE OLD TESTAMENT

As THE reader looks back on the Sapiential Books of the Old Testament some questions are likely to occur to him — questions perhaps not fully formed, but at least implicit to the literature he has been reading. In this final chapter we propose to anticipate some of these questions and to point the way to their solutions.

What is Wisdom?

One of these questions is disarmingly simple: What is Old Testament Wisdom? But the answer, as is now apparent, is exceedingly complex; there is no one answer, for there are many facets to the concept of wisdom. It is the skill of a craftsman (Eccl 10:10), such as that of the men who made Aaron's vestments (Ex 28:3) or of Beseleel who had a "divine spirit of skill and understanding and knowledge in every craft: in the production of embroidery, in making things of gold, silver or bronze, in cutting and mounting precious stones, in carving wood" (Ex 31:3–5). A wise man is one who has a future ahead of him (Prv 23:18; 24:14) because he knows how to live; wisdom is old age, i.e., the experience and knowledge acquired by age (Jb 12:12). The wise man is the adviser of kings (Prv 31:1; Sir 39:4) and the teacher of the simple (Prv 1:8; Sir 51:23). Wisdom has to do with diligence in one's labor, honesty, and the natural virtues, as well as with shrewdness in action (Prv 14:15). Finally, "the beginning of wisdom is fear of the Lord" (Prv 1:7; Sir 1:9 ff.), because wisdom hates evil (Prv 8:13) and leads to friendship with God (Wis 7:14).

Wisdom is all these things — and more. Wisdom is portrayed with an air of mystery, of remoteness from man. She is essentially with God and apart from man. We may recall here the texts about her inaccessibility, which we examined above.

No one knows the way to wisdom except God (Jb 28:23). Coheleth asked, "who can find it out?" (Eccl 7:24), and Sirach put the same question and answered it clearly:

> To whom has wisdom's root been revealed?
>   Who knows her subtleties?
> There is but one, wise and truly awe-inspiring,
>   seated upon his throne;
> It is the Lord; he created her,
>   has seen her and taken note of her (1:5–7).

This inaccessibility of wisdom is akin to another important characteristic: she is personified as though she were a divine being.

This aspect of wisdom, which we have reserved until now for fuller treatment, is described at great length in Proverbs 8, Sirach 24, and Wisdom 7. At first sight it is no great surprise to read that wisdom is divine. If man is wise, God is all-wise. Yet there is no other quality of Yahweh which is elaborated at such length as his wisdom. And in this process wisdom is personified in a manner that goes far beyond other Old Testament personifications, such as Word or Spirit.

In Proverbs 8 wisdom is personified in a modest way as Dame Wisdom in verses 1–21. This is a continuation of the same literary personification initiated in 1:20 ff. and found also in 9:1–18 where she is contrasted with Dame Folly. But in 8:22–31 wisdom is associated with God in an unusually intimate fashion:

> The Lord begot me, the firstborn of his ways,
>   the forerunner of his prodigies of long ago;
> From of old I was poured forth,
>   at the first, before the earth.
> When there were no depths I was brought forth,
>   when there were no fountains or springs of water. . . .
> When he established the heavens I was there,
>   when he marked out the vault over the face of the deep. . . .
> Then was I beside him as his craftsman,
>   and I was his delight day by day.

Playing before him all the while,
  playing on the surface of his earth
  [and I found delight in the sons of men].

Yahweh "begot" wisdom; she was "poured forth" — and this "from
of old." It is as close as the Hebrew writer can get to our notion of
eternity. She is "firstborn," "forerunner," "before the hills" (the
very hills that are called timeless in Gn 49:26). When creation began she was there to watch it (vv. 27–29), and she even had a role
in the creative activity as "craftsman" of God, bringing him delight
by her activity. (That "she found delight in the sons of men"
may be a gloss, added in the light of Sir 24:8 ff.; the purpose of
the brackets in the CCD translation is to suggest that the line,
which disturbs the rhythm of the verse, is a gloss.) Finally, her
work does not stop with creation; she is to bring men to God:

> For he who finds me finds life,
>   and wins favor from the Lord (8:35).

In the twenty-fourth chapter of Sirach the discourse on wisdom
likewise begins with her creation:

> From the mouth of the Most High I came forth,
>   and mistlike covered the earth (24:3).

But Sirach conceives of her function differently than the author
of Proverbs; no sooner does she exist than she seeks a place to
dwell in:

> Over waves of the sea, over all the land,
>   over every people and nation I held sway.
> Among all these I sought a resting place;
>   in whose inheritance should I abide?
> Then the Creator of all gave me his command,
>   and he who formed me chose the spot for my tent,
> Saying, "In Jacob make your dwelling,
>   in Israel your inheritance."
> Before all ages, in the beginning, he created me,
>   and through all ages I shall not cease to be.

In the holy Tent I ministered before him,
and in Sion I fixed my abode.
Thus in the chosen city he has given me rest,
in Jerusalem is my domain.
I have struck root among the glorious people,
in the portion of the Lord, his heritage (24:6–12).

Yahweh bade her to take up residence among his Chosen People, Jacob, and she dwelt in the Holy City of Jerusalem, beautiful and stately (vv. 13–17), offering her fruits to the people (vv. 18–21). Who is this wisdom? Sirach identifies her unequivocally:

All this is true of the book of the Most High's covenant,
the law which Moses commanded us
as an inheritance for the community of Jacob (24:22).

Wisdom is the Torah, the "books of Moses."

The author of the book of Wisdom describes wisdom as "the artificer of all" (7:22; cf. the "craftsman" in Prv 8:30), who teaches all things to man. This is no difficult task for her since "she penetrates and pervades all things by reason of her purity" (7:24).

For she is an aura of the might of God
and a pure effusion of the glory of the Almighty;
therefore nought that is sullied enters into her.
For she is the refulgence of eternal light,
the spotless mirror of the power of God,
the image of his goodness.
And she, who is one, can do all things,
and renews everything while herself perduring;
And passing into holy souls from age to age,
she produces friends of God and prophets.
For there is nought God loves, be it not one who dwells with
Wisdom (7:25–28).

Thus the divine nature of wisdom is once more affirmed, and many divine attributes are ascribed to her: she originates from God; she is all-powerful and all-holy; she shares in the creation and government of the world. Are we to conclude that in these passages wisdom is actually an hypostasis, a Person? This is difficult to admit in a Jewish monotheist. Exaggeration or extremes in personification do not mean that the Jews recognized wisdom as a divine person apart from God. Rather, it is more fruitful to approach this portrayal of wisdom from another angle, that of communication. God is so taken with his creation that he communicates himself to it, and this communication is wisdom. She "produces friends of God" (7:27); she is an "unfailing treasure" which will win for men "the friendship of God" (7:14). This idea of God's communicating something of himself to man is capable of development; just what does he communicate over and above the gifts of creation? It is hard to escape the conclusion, if one accepts the continuity between the Old Testament and the New, that God is preparing mankind for the Incarnation of Christ. St. Paul recognized this when he termed Christ "the Wisdom of God" (1 Cor 1:24), "the image of the invisible God, the firstborn of every creature" (Col 1:15). St. John, in particular, betrays the influence of the Old Testament teaching on Wisdom. He has patterned the prologue to his gospel (1:1–18) on the sequence of thought which is found in the description of personified Wisdom. Wisdom describes herself in the following order: her close relation to God, her role in creation, her dwelling among men, and the benefits she brings to men. This movement is reflected in the description of the *Logos* or Word: the Word was in the beginning in close relationship to God (in fact, was God, 1:1), and had a role in creation (everything was made by him, 1:3); he came into the world (1:10 ff.) and brought the grace of sonship (1:12), and grace and truth (1:17 f.).

Finally, we may point out a characteristic of Hebrew thought which we have noted before (in relation to Yahweh's causality and man's free will). Typical of Old Testament thought are the conflicting concepts of wisdom, with no attempt to resolve them. We cannot categorize them in our western mode of thinking without doing violence to the Jewish teaching. Thus, wisdom is the Law (Sir), but also divine, begotten of God (Prv, Wis). No contradiction is felt, and none should be seen here: the tension between created and uncreated wisdom is simply allowed to remain.

The Wisdom Movement

We situated the origins of the wisdom literature in the court life of Israel. The Israelites were conscious that this was an area of thought not proper to themselves, and the wisdom movement in the beginning was patterned on the Egyptian plan. Hence there is no reference in the preexilic material of Proverbs to the Law, or the saving events of the books of Exodus, Josue, etc. To that extent, the early wisdom literature was not distinctively Israelite. But it would be shortsighted to say that it was not religious. It was not only religious but informed by the typically Israelite understanding of Yahweh, the God of Israel. What was borrowed and also what was the fruit of personal observation were largely re-thought and assimilated so as to become a reflection of a Yahwist point of view. This specifically Israelite touch can be seen in proverbs like the following:

> Like a stream is the king's heart in the hand of the Lord;
> wherever it pleases him, he directs it (Prv 21.1).

> There is no wisdom, no understanding,
> no counsel, against the Lord (Prv 21:30).

But if its origins are pre-exilic, the wisdom movement in Israel is essentially a postexilic phenomenon; practically all of the extant literature must be dated after the exile. The prophetic activity was coming to an end with the restoration of the Jewish community at the end of the sixth century B.C., and the role of the scribe or teacher, the man who knew the Law, came to the fore. The practical business of how to live and how to "fear the Lord" needed to be stated and developed. The first nine chapters of the book of Proverbs exemplifies the style and hortatory manner of this teaching.

Along with the wisdom movement went a renewed interest in the sacred traditions of earlier history, as the compilation of the Pentateuch shows. There is an interesting comment on wisdom in Deuteronomy 4:5–6:

Therefore, I teach you the statutes and decrees as the Lord, my God, commanded me, that you may observe them in the land you are entering to occupy. Observe them carefully, for thus will you give evidence of your wisdom and intelligence to the nations, who will hear of all these statutes and say, "This great nation is truly a wise and intelligent people."

It is noteworthy that the reference is to something specifically their own, not the wisdom literature which all nations share in, that stamps the people as wise and intelligent in the eyes of the nations. With the completion of the Law and the Prophets the Jews had become "the People of the Book," and scribes and teachers, of whom Sirach is the most outstanding example, were needed for the religious education of the young. Yet there is not a strong national or institutional coloring to the wisdom movement. Of all the books, Ecclesiasticus and Wisdom (although the latter goes far beyond Sirach as regards retribution) can be rightly considered as the most traditionalist. Yet their references to national institutions and concepts are relatively infrequent. In both there are historical sections, but outside of these there is hardly an explicit reference to anything national, such as covenant, cult, election, etc. The broad and somewhat moralizing trend of the wisdom movement remains.

It might appear that the author of Job and even Coheleth are somewhat tangential to the wisdom movement. They are "problem" writers, occupied with the paradox of the just man who suffers, the ultimate meaning of life. But these problems are only acute, particular formulations of the material handed down and discussed by the sages. The usual teaching was concerned with God's government of the world in the present (not the past) and man's way of life in that world. Both Job and Coheleth represent a new and daring approach — an experiential approach — to these questions, but it is all in the wisdom tradition. Coheleth (or at least a disciple) reminds us: "Besides being wise, Coheleth taught the people knowledge, and weighed, scrutinized and arranged many proverbs" (12:9). The book of Job has included many teachings that formed part of the typical lessons given by a sage. One may compare the description of God's power and majesty in Job 12:7 ff. and 36:22 ff. with Sirach 42:15 ff. The sage who composed Job betrays his calling in many typical wisdom statements; Job and the three Friends reason like sages.

The International Character of Wisdom

The international aspect of wisdom literature has been stressed above, especially in the chapter concerning Proverbs, where the Instruction of Amen-em-Ope, the Egyptian, was discussed. Are there other extra-biblical parallels to the wisdom of Israel?

As for the gnomic sayings found in the book of Proverbs, it will surprise no one that this type of wisdom is found in almost every literature and civilization. In the immediate area of Israel we have many Egyptian and Akkadian proverbs. The famous Wisdom of Ahiqar (Ahiqar is mentioned in the book of Tobias, 1:22; 2:10; 11:17; 14:20, Greek numbering) has long been known in its Aramaic form and in translation. The story concerns the betrayal of Ahiqar by a nephew he has befriended, and his eventual restoration to his post as chancellor during the reign of Esarhaddon of Assyria. To his nephew, Ahiqar delivers two addresses which contain the typical maxims of proverb literature: such commonplaces as disciplining children for their own good, guarding one's tongue, care in dealing with the king, honoring secrets that have been entrusted, etc. The last twenty-five years have witnessed the publication of many ancient Sumerian proverbs (the Sumerian culture of the third millennium B.C. preceded the Akkadian in Mesopotamia) which are similar in style and content to the wisdom sayings of the rest of the Fertile Crescent.

The problem type of wisdom literature, such as Job and Coheleth, is also represented in the ancient world. However, the similarity should not be exaggerated; it seems unfair to speak of a Babylonian Job and a Babylonian Coheleth because they fall far behind their biblical counterparts.

The work of the Babylonian Job is known as *Ludlul Bel Nemeqi* ("I will praise the Lord of Wisdom") and has been read and studied for half a century. Its theme is the suffering of a just man, who soliloquizes throughout the poem. The beginning is not extant, but the author is portrayed lamenting bitterly over his suffering. Whereas he was once a lord, he is now a slave, sighing by day and weeping by night at the evil that oppresses him. Prayer is useless; priests and oracles are impotent — as though he had been irreligious or failed to perform his duties to God and man. Actually he had been meticulously exact about his religion. So he complains:

> Oh that I only knew that these things are well pleasing
>   to a god!
> What is good in one's sight is evil for a god,
> What is bad in one's own mind is good for his god.
> Who can understand the counsel of the gods in the
>   midst of heaven?
> The plan of a god is deep waters, who can comprehend it?
> Where has befuddled mankind ever learned what a god's
>   conduct is?

In a series of dreams he is healed, as heavenly messengers appear to him. The work itself is hardly worth comparing with Job. What is more significant is that it seems to be an example of a literary tradition concerning the suffering of the just. In 1952 another piece of this type of literature, also Babylonian, was published, and a few years later Sumerian fragments which seem to deal with the same theme became known, so that some scholars speak of a Sumerian Job. While the drift of this literature is not yet in clear focus, all these examples suggest that the author of Job adapted an accepted literary form, long current in the Semitic world. But it should be added that no one before or since has surpassed his treatment.

There is also the work of a Babylonian Ecclesiastes, an acrostic poem called "A dialogue about human misery." But there is more than one example of this type of literature in Mesopotamia. We have also the "Pessimistic Dialogue," a conversation between a master and his servant. In this piece a master proposes to do a certain thing and his servant points out all the benefits and good points of this action. Then the master changes his mind and the slave agrees, pointing out the bad features of what he had formerly praised. As an example, this is what he says about women:

> "Servant, obey me." Yes, my lord, yes. "A woman will I love." Yes, love, my lord, love. The man who loves a woman forgets pain and trouble. "No, servant, a woman I shall not love." [do not love,] my lord, do not [love]. Woman is a well, woman is an iron dagger — a sharp one! — which cuts a man's neck.

The dialogue ranges over several topics and always the vanity, in terms of advantages and disadvantages, is brought out. However, none of these literary works capture the spirit of Coheleth, and the comparison is all in his favor.

These are the more classic examples of extra-biblical parallels to the Old Testament wisdom literature. Because the Israelite writers were very much a part of the civilization and culture in which they lived, they imitated and adapted what they found at hand. The past fifty years of archaeological research have proved that in a magnificent manner and helped us to understand Israel better. This approach is being furthered by constant research and we can expect the list of parallels to grow. For example, there exists some evidence for a Canaanite background to Proverbs 8 (the personification of divine wisdom). Since Canaanite background for so many portions of the Psalms and other Old Testament works has been clearly shown, it is at least plausible that this influence may be found in Proverbs 8. It is precisely along these lines of illustrating biblical material from non-biblical literature that the greatest progress has been made in recent biblical study.

Revelation and the Wisdom Literature

The stress laid on the international aspect of the wisdom literature and on the parallels between Israel and her neighbors may cause uneasiness for some readers. In what respect is the Bible different from other ancient Semitic literature? How can it be the word of God, and yet be so terribly human? These questions have arisen in every area where biblical writings have been compared to

contemporary extra-biblical sources. We will consider a few principles fundamental to a correct understanding of the Bible and
then address ourselves to the wisdom literature in particular.

When we say that the Bible is inspired we mean that God is
the Author of the Bible; he obviously had the co-operation of a
human author, such as Sirach or the author of Job. The nature
of the influence which God exerted on this human instrument is
a mystery, as is any action of God upon man's faculties (one
thinks of the influence we call actual grace). But we are able to
establish certain facts about this influence. The first fact, very pertinent to the question we have raised, is that God's influence allowed this man to employ his abilities in a normal manner. If he
was a brilliant poet, he remained that, no more no less. If he
wrote poetry poorly, his literary ability was neither improved nor
lessened by God's influence. Whether he was an independent
thinker, or a collector of other people's thoughts, God made whatever use of him he could; he respected his abilities and used them
accordingly. God's influence upon the human author was exerted
in such a way he did not necessarily know that he was inspired.
Nor did this action of God spare him from working long and
hard in the production of his book (cf. 2 Mc 2:19–32).

Second, this inspiring action of God which has to do with the
production of a written work is not to be confused with revelation.
Revelation means that God communicated certain ideas, especially
those beyond man's natural ability to know, to a person who may
or may not have ever written a line. The manner of this communication may be by way of a spiritual experience, a spiritual
intuition, such as may be presumed with many of the great
prophets. Or the communication might consist in a quite rational
insight, an illumination that moves a man to grasp a truth that
has been only dimly seen or hinted at in a previous generation (we
shall return to this in connection with the doctrine of immortality).
There are many other possible modes of communication. But in all
this, revelation is really antecedent to any inspiring influence of
God; revelation is one *possible* source for the knowledge that an
inspired writer has.

Finally, how are we to conceive of revelation in the case of an inspired writer? Perhaps the most common misconception is to imagine that the Lord simply pumped ideas and words into the somewhat empty mind of the writer; then we would have the sheer ideas and words of God. The Old Testament itself suggests that the Lord has never done that. In even the most exalted supernatural visions that have been described in the Bible, the writer expresses what he has learned in *his* way under the influence of God's inspiration. God has respected the nature of his instrument and allowed the human author to react to the divine communication, to express the divine message in words and imagery that are part of his culture. Hence there is no reason to wonder at the use of Canaanite or Egyptian themes and ideas which enter into the composition of the Bible. The human author remains subject to the various literary and cultural influences of his time; the voice of Isaias is not that of Jeremias.

As far as the Sapiential Books are concerned, we do not mean to imply that there is no revelation of God communicated in them. As a matter of fact, God has progressively and gradually revealed the idea of a blessed immortality in precisely these books of the Old Testament. But the communication was not a static, frozen announcement. The Jews did not suddenly become aware overnight, as it were, that now a "heaven" with God existed. It is important to keep in mind that revelation in the era before Christ was not a declaration by an infallible teaching authority. The synagogue was not the Apostolic Body of the Church, and we cannot transfer the notion of a teaching magisterium into the Old Testament period. Today the magisterium of the Church defines for Christians what God has revealed; there is a certain orderliness and clarity in the statements of the Popes and the Councils. But let us not transpose our mentality with that of Israel.

Rather, the revelation of a blessed immortality was a subtle and delicate process. As we have seen, the Hebrew concept of Sheol was a formidable barrier to their thought about the next life; it was close to nonexistence. But it came to be felt as a paradox, the more Israel knew about Yahweh. Here was a God who had chosen them as his possession, who dwelt among his People in the holy city, who promised them *life* in return for their fidelity, who had indicated a great destiny in store for his People. Could a God such as this let all that *hesed,* that loyal, loving kindness, come to an end with death? Was the fate in Sheol commensurate to a God who made such touching overtures to men? One senses the extreme disappointment in the common complaint that in Sheol an Israelite will no longer be able to praise God.

The paradox of such a God and such a destiny is put in sharper focus in the problem literature of Job and Coheleth. They are trying to find a satisfying answer in this life, and they hardly succeed. But they prepare the way, by their defeat, for God's revelation. The Hebrew understanding of God is slowly ripening to such a point that some psalmists understand that Yahweh will never let them go. They have no knowledge of what this really means, but the fact is there to console them. They have no fancy phrases about a future life, but their God will redeem them "from the power of the nether world by receiving" them (Ps 49:16); with him they shall always be (Ps 73:23).

What is it that makes this union between Yahweh and his faithful servant indissoluble? The Book of Wisdom spells out the answer: justice — justice is immortal (Wis 1:15). What will it ultimately mean if this union between Yahweh and the pious Israelite is to persevere? It means that the individual will join the ranks of the Lord's heavenly court: "accounted among the sons of God" — "his lot is with the saints" (Wis 5:5). Thus a future life of blessed immortality developed into a triumphant affirmation, as God slowly illumined the minds of his servants and gave them insight into himself and his designs. In this consideration we have left much unsaid; we cannot capture the precise moments of revelation. There is another approach which we will simply mention: the full-blown belief in the resurrection of the body which appears in Daniel 12:2, and which was a motivating force in the days of the Maccabees (2 Mc 7:1 ff.). This belief found expression in the "period of the martyrs," when Jews were dying for their faith during the persecution of Antiochus Epiphanes and his successors.

The doctrine of blessed immortality is only one example of revelation at work in the Old Testament. It is hardly necessary to add that many other developments of revealed doctrine could be instanced: sin, Messianism, etc.

On the other hand, there is much in the Sapiential Books that neither demands nor betrays any supernatural revelation. Certainly there are many conclusions concerning human affairs which could have been and were in fact reached by an Egyptian or Canaanite as well as by a Hebrew. Much of Proverbs 10 ff., and of the book of Sirach (e.g., the table etiquette of Sir 31:12 ff.) belongs to the common heritage of the ancient East. These teachings represent the body of traditional advice handed down from generation to generation among the scribes; this was the scholastic material that educated young men would be expected to know. It was within the designs of God's Providence that this be preserved and put down in writing — to be included among the books which he inspired.

As it appears, there would be little or no revelation necessary on God's part. However, God's influence is not easily measured; one cannot just write off any portion of the Bible as not having its roots, at least, in revelation. Because one cannot in all honesty level the Israelite point of view with that of the Egyptian or any other of his neighbors. The Israelite view is necessarily orientated by a position founded in the revelation of Yahweh to Israel. There is an essentially Yahwistic context in which the sacred writer judged and interpreted the wisdom of the ancient world. He understood in his own way whatever he borrowed and inherited.

CONCLUSION

THIS book cannot come to an end without making a final suggestion primarily concerning the New Testament. One who has carefully read the wisdom books of the Old Testament may well expect to hear echoes which he may not have heard before when he turns to the words of Jesus in the New Testament, because Jesus, too, followed in the tradition of the Old Testament wisdom teacher. Concerning him people asked in admiration and puzzlement, "What is this wisdom that is given him?" (Mk 6:2.) And Jesus compared himself to the ideal sage when he said that the Queen of the South "came from the ends of the earth to hear the wisdom of Solomon, and behold, there is more than Solomon here" (Mt 12:42).

The basic observations about Hebrew parallelism which were made in the first chapter are applicable to the New Testament as well. Very many of the discourses of Jesus are cast in this familiar rhythm:

> There is nothing hidden that will not be made manifest;
> nor is anything concealed that will not come to light
> (Mk 4:22).

> For he who would save his life will lose it,
> but he who loses his life for my sake . . . will save it
> (Mk 8:35).

The parables of Jesus are very similar to the proverbs that we have been examining in the wisdom writers. This similarity can be seen in the style, for the New Testament parable corresponds to the Old Testament *mashal:*

Do not lay up for yourselves treasures on earth,
    where rust and moth consume,
    and where thieves break in and steal;
but lay up for yourselves treasures in heaven,
    where neither rust nor moth consumes,
    nor thieves break in and steal.
For where your treasure is, there your heart also will be
                            (Mt 6:19 ff.; cf. Job 22:24 ff.).

More important than mere style is the continuity of the wisdom tradition in the Old and New Testaments. The wisdom teaching reaches a climax in the doctrine of Jesus. "Every scribe instructed in the kingdom of heaven is like a householder who brings out of his storeroom things new and old" (Mt 13:52). While the teaching of Christ cannot be reduced to the pattern of Israelite wisdom teaching, Jesus did bring out "things new and old." He inherited the Old Testament teaching, only to deepen and expand it. For example, when his disciples asked him, "Rabbi, who has sinned, this man or his parents, that he should be born blind?" (Jn 9:2), we hear the question of Job all over again. We have already seen how Coheleth's judgment on the values of this world lead up to the question which Christ asked, "What does it profit a man . . .?" (Mt 16:26). An interesting example of the manner in which Christ touches on the dilemma of Job and Coheleth is to be found in Mt 5:45: our Father in heaven "makes his sun rise on the good and evil, and sends rain on the just and unjust." The bitter complaint of the two Hebrew thinkers — that God does not intervene to punish the evil and reward the good in this life — is quietly and simply admitted. But this fact is used to suggest the mysterious mercy of the Father in heaven: a mercy that is at least as mysterious as the problem of evil. With Job and Coheleth, Jesus indicates that suffering in this world is not a necessary index of sin (Jn 9:1 ff.; Lk 13:1 ff.). However, unlike them, Jesus speaks of a future world "where neither rust nor moth consumes. . . ."

It is precisely with regard to the future world and immortality that the teaching of Jesus caps the trend of thought in the wisdom

books. The constant preoccupation of the sage with life is matched
by the teaching on eternal life in the New Testament. Even if the
author of the book of Wisdom arrived at a belief in a blessed immortality, it is easy to see that his notion is only a faint, if brilliant,
approximation to the New Testament reality of union with God
in Christ through the glorious resurrection.

INDEX*

---

* The individual books we have discussed are set in capitals.

161